JUSTIN,

It's Not My Fault

RICK CAIN

Justin, It's Not My Fault

Copyright © 2019 Rick Cain

ISBN: 978-0-359-72803-9 (pbk)

First Edition

About the Author

I was born in Canada and I'm a citizen of Canada only. I was raised by parents who lived understanding the perils of a world war, who also lived through a recession. I was brought up with the understanding that nothing is free, and raised my children the same way. We were told that with an education and a good work ethic you would succeed in life. I was fortunate enough to acquire multiple trades and affordably raise a family in a rural setting. There was no such thing as subsidized daycare, but a single family income allowed one of the family members to raise the children at home. There was no such thing as subsidized or free secondary education. My son's education and expenses while in school were paid for by his parents. There was no such thing as affordable housing, home ownership subsidies or grants to upgrade your own home. Mortgages were at 13% interest and you required a 25% down-payment to purchase a house. You could only obtain a vehicle loan if you met the banking criteria (i.e. had a job). Employment wasn't an issue as numerous jobs were available, but you couldn't sit waiting for one to come to you. I personally worked coast to coast to maintain a quality of life for myself and my family. I was frequently away from home, often for long periods of time. To maintain a family relationship they were able to travel with me during some summer months. At one time I considered myself to be upper-middle class. Today my work requirements for having to travel away from home have not changed but my income now places me amongst the middle class, at best. I am fortunate enough to belong to a pension plan but the way new taxes are constantly being introduced and increased, I wonder if it will support me with the lifestyle I worked my entire life for.

I have affiliation to no single political party. I have always, up until now, voted both provincially and federally according to election platforms.

Every generation has had fears that that their grandchildren will face tough times. The most significant reason I created this book is because I have a Caucasian grandson and granddaughter who will never see entitlements and will be forever penalized simply because of who their ancestors were.

Table of Contents

Introduction
Open transparent government
Create a Better Life for Canadians
Canadian Citizenship and Immigration
Gender Equality
Indigenous Relations
- 2016 Federal budget
- 2016/17 Federal budget
- 2017/18 Federal budget
- Crown Indigenous and Northern Affairs 2018 budget
- Indigenous Services Canada 2018/19 budget
- Reconciliation
- Infrastructure
- Educational and Employment Opportunities
- Health
- Justice
- Climate change
Author's Closing Remarks

Introduction

It is my intention through this book to show, item-by-item, how Justin Trudeau and his Liberal party majority government have over 2 ½ years undermined Canadian values and pitted Canadian against Canadian and province against province. This book is not meant to be racist, anti-immigrant or prejudiced. Indigenous, Inuit, Metis and refugees cannot be chastised for taking advantage of a flawed government system. Immigration is needed for this country but in the legitimate, legal way. In many cases Indigenous people deserve compensation for past practise but the pendulum has swung too far—to the point where privilege has exceeded rights. Canada has been built by our immigrant forefathers and mothers. Everyone deserves an equal opportunity for a job, but qualifications should be the determining factor for employment. This book simply reuses and reemphasizes previously published articles from the media. The wording of the original articles has been shortened in length but not changed in context. At times articles may seem repetitive but it is only to reemphasize differences between news articles.

Justin Trudeau promised us "Sunny Days Ahead". He promised to create jobs, lower taxes and create a better life for the middle class. In his election platform of 2015 stated he would add $26 billion to the Canadian debt but balance the books by 2019. The Liberal Government in 2016-17 increased debt by $25.5 billion, in 2017-18 by $24.4 billion and 2018-19 predict $19.6 billion. We are presently on pace with his leadership to add a total of $127 billion to the Canadian debt by 2024 if re-elected, and no predicted date for balanced books. What he has actually delivered to Canadians was his own ideologies, reneged promises, reckless overspending, and blatant arrogance. It is through Justin Trudeau's use of certain words that his political career has escalated but at the same time divided the country. Those words being racism, feminism, Islamophobia, equality, hate crimes, colonialism and fear mongering. All of these things have damaged our "Constitutional Right" to freedom of speech. Racism of today is fuelled by jealousy, greed, favouritism and entitlements. Justin Trudeau has allowed the United Nations to dictate to Canada how to best govern our own country with Indigenous and immigration issues being the most obvious examples.

I applaud the Thunder Bay Chronicle Journal for their news coverage and seemingly unbiased approach to journalism, compared to the articles published from larger urban area newspapers. Be it published news, radio or television coverage in Canada it is my opinion that censorship and favouritism are blatantly shown toward the Liberal agenda. Canadian broadcasting has been funded over $1 billion annually by the Federal Government and additional funding being made available. In many cases the media reports concentrate on a one-sided view of events and fails to communicate the entire story to the public. Over 90% of the itemized transcripts in this book have been extracted from the Thunder Bay Chronicle Journal daily newspaper which will show with the date printed and "CJ" A second reference commonly used shows as 'Frontier Centre" with is actually the Frontier Centre for Public Policy. This is an independent think tank with offices in Alberta, Saskatchewan and Manitoba. Their research is to analyze current affairs and public policy, then develop effective and meaningful ideas for good governance and reform. As an organization they do not subscribe to any political ideology, seek or accept any government funding.

The present government's Socialist agenda is to provide every Canadian with the same entitlements, (housing, health care and essentials) whether you're middle class, poor, working or unemployed. Justin Trudeau has been infatuated with the fact that with his majority government he is entitled to monetarily reimburse citizens for what their party consider historical wrongs. Each of these payouts has been delivered without any legal prosecution to perpetrators. This makes only the taxpayer once again responsible for everything. He has compensated people at the expense of present and future generations, for what was considered rightful practice during that time period in history. This book is intended to show how individual groups are singled out and given special privileges, benefits and entitlements simply to buy their votes at election time. A practice used since the start of democracy but blatantly misused by the present government.

The Federal government has constantly put emphasis on how good our democratic legal system is. In the last 2 1/2 years there have been countless times individual "appointed" Federal court judges have enforced rulings that have overridden elected governments decisions, which affect Canada's entire population. Allowing lawyers to represent clients and be reimbursed when a court makes a monetary ruling, has produced nothing but "ambulance chasers".

In the name of populating the country statistic show that mainstream Canadians are having on average 1.5 children per family, not counting families with no children. This is true mainly due to the fact, that it is all they can afford. Canadians that work and pay taxes support the have-nots and people that for whatever reason are unemployed or unemployable. Pro-rated child care benefits are the greatest example of penalizing the "willing to work" middle-class Canadians.

I am hoping this book will act as a wake-up call to all Canadians that fail to follow politics and to those people that are self-committed to a (there's nothing I can do attitude). It's time to try and regain common sense and accountability to this country for the sake of future generations. Canadians are known to have short memories and easily bought off at election time with false promises to support people's own self interests.

Throughout this book there are many monetary values that are in the billions of dollars. Most people have no comprehension as to what a billion dollars actually is. If you really want Politicians looking after your money here are examples of what a billion is; If you handed out $1 per second, 24 hours a day, 7 days a week for 31 years you still would not have handed out 1 billion dollars. One billion seconds ago it was 1959.

Open, Transparent Government

Jan 4/17 "National Post"

At the end of 2015 Justin Trudeau suspended The First Nations Financial Transparency Act. This allowed a provision that Ottawa could withhold federal funds for any band that failed to publish audited statements and a list of what Chiefs and Band Councillors were paid.

Feb 28/17 "CJ"

The Liberal government has budgeted **$1.3 billion over 5 years.** to meet a United Nations commitment to protect 17% of its land and inland waters by 2020

Mar 21/17 "Maclean's"

The cost of The Trudeau trip to Aga Khan's island was **$127,000**. Approximately $72,000 was for the RCMP security detail. Security rules don't allow Justin Trudeau to fly on anything but government aircraft yet he took a personal flight to the island on Aga Khan's helicopter. For the holiday trip Trudeau reimbursed the taxpayer for the costs of commercial flights which came to **$4,895.94.** That 3 hour government aircraft flight valued at $32,000 plus an additional $1,720.37 for food, beverages, taxes etc.

Mar 22/17 "The Star"

The increase in sin taxes will put an additional $55 million from tobacco and $30 million from alcohol into government coffers in 2017-18 fiscal year.

May 9/17 "CJ"

The "Federal Firearms Bill" [now the *Firearms Act]* will allow the RCMP the ability to classify semi-automatic, restricted and non-restricted firearms but does not classify assault weapons. Ralph Goodale has pledged **$327 million** over 5 years and an additional **$100 million** per year after toward gun control.

July 7/17 "CJ"

Justin Trudeau publicly stated he didn't recall the event after a past conflict was brought out. Rose Knight confirmed that she was the reporter that Justin had groped 18 years. ago. This appeared in an article in the Creston Valley Advance Newspaper at the time.

Oct 6/17 "CJ"

Justin Trudeau said Canadians voted for a carbon solution. He says Canadians gave him a mandate to implement a carbon tax.

Nov 14/17 "CJ"

The Federal government spent $827 million on a used icebreaker that was originally supposed to cost $610 million. Officials failed to realize there would be a $217 million cost for tariffs, brokerage fees, engineering and costs to make the boat seaworthy.

Nov 24/17 "CJ"

At the Charlottetown Confederation Centre Justin Trudeau targeted income equality and tax evasion. He stated it is unfair for parents to have to decide if they can afford boots for their children when CEO's are making $ millions in bonuses. Ottawa has committed $1 billion to investigate offshore tax evasion.

Dec 17/17 "CJ"

A "Fairness in Petroleum Pricing Act brought forward by the NDP was defeated by the majority Liberal government before it could go to second reading. This was meant to regulate fuel prices from the vast differences that exist.

Dec 7/17 "CJ"

The Federal Government after criticism from the previous year's summer grant applications has revamped the wording for 2017. From applicants having to declare themselves supportive of abortion rights to declare that they don't infringe on any Canadian legal right when funding of summer projects is applied for.

Dec 10/17 "CTV News"

Veterans are waiting in a backlog of approximately 29,000 applications for funding. Veterans Affairs Minister Sheamus O'Regan says action is being taken and hundreds of additional staff will be hired. More streamlining will happen and Veterans will be given more benefit of doubt on applications.

Dec 20/17 "Globe and Mail"

Ethics Commissioner Mary Dawson ruled that Prime Minister Justin Trudeau broke 4 rules of Canada's ethics law over 2 all-expense paid family trips to the Bahamas. Not only did Trudeau and his family vacation at Aga Khan's residence at Christmas in 2014 but his wife took a separate vacation there in March 2016 as well. The PM. stated he was allowed to receive gifts from friends but it was proven that he and Aga Khan had only spoken to each other once 30 years prior. Aga Khan is a billionaire spiritual leader of the worlds Ismaili Muslims. Discussions were under way for a **$15 million** federal grant toward an endowment fund, for the "Global Centre for Pluralism" (founded by Aga Khan).

Dec 4/17 "Global News"

The Federal government will hike liquor taxes by 2% this year and hike it every year after in line with inflation. By doing this the tax increases will no longer be tabled in budgets. Canadians already pay taxes at 80% for spirits, 65-70% on wine and 50% on beer.

Nov 28/17 "Globe and Mail"

Controversy over Bill Morneau's selling shares in Morneau Shepell days before making a government announcement toward new tax brackets. This could have an effect on the value of shares in his company.

Dec 18/17 "The Star"

Ottawa will spend **$80 million** to research and study the prevention, containment and minimization of environmental damage from oil spills. $44.5 million for scientist and research collaboration worldwide $16.8 million to fund scientists and provide new equipment, $17.1 million to enhance ocean wind and wave models, and $1.5 million towards development of an ocean protection plan.

Feb 1/18 "CTV News"

Justin Trudeau openly commented saying that "some vets want more than the government can afford.

May 16/18 "Globe and Mail"

Justin Trudeau is bragging that his Cabinet contains more Sikh's than Mr. Modi's Cabinet in India. Canada has 4 Sikh Ministers but proportionately the Sikh's only make up 1.5% of Canada's total population. Indo Canadians make up for 4% of the population therefore there are twice as many Muslims as Sikhs.

June 5/18 "National Post"

The Phoenix Pay System has cost taxpayers upwards of **$1.1 billion** and could cost as much as **$2.5 billion over 5 years.** Carla Qualtrough estimates by 2019, 25% of Federal Services pay will be stabilized. Since 2016 Canada's 300,000 public servants have been overpaid, underpaid or have had botched tax forms. This system was supposed to save $70 million per year but has exceeded prior costs by $230 million per year. A study has been implemented to find a replacement and a timeframe for a possible replacement. The Liberal government has committed to spending **$16 million** over 2 years. to build a new pay system.

June 22/18 "Calgary Herald"

Ottawa has readjusted the equalization payments to Provinces. By instituting Bill C-74 equalization will pay $60 per capita to Provinces that suddenly lose 5% of their revenue. This would be a loss from other than renewable resources. In the case of Alberta, the drop in oil revenue is irrelevant as to equalization income, yet is still included in the wealth calculation.

Nov 12/18 "CJ"

Prior to electoral defeat the Conservative

government predicted a $262.2 billion deficit but a $1.4 billion surplus for 2015-16. The Liberal deficit after 2016-17 was $291.4 billion; an increase of $18.2 billion The Liberal deficit after 2019-20 is predicted to be $321 billion. **From 2015 to 2020 the deficit has increased 22%**

Dec 4/18 "CJ"
        Gun control activists are impatient to pass Bill C-71. In part this bill will allow authorities to investigate a person's life history versus a 5 year background check.

Dec 19/18 "Canadian Press"
        The Liberal government has unveiled **$595 million** in fresh funding to subsidize Canadian news outlets.

Dec 20/18 "World News"
        The Liberals have approved a tax reimbursement of $14.7 million for canceling the Northern Gateway pipeline. The cancelation of the pipeline was due to the fact that the Liberal government banned tankers carrying large amounts of crude oil from traveling the British Columbia's northern coast.

Jan 9/19 "CBC News"
        Justin Trudeau was criticized for filming a Liberal fundraising video in his office on Parliament Hill. According to the House of Commons, politicians cannot use parliamentary premises for partisan purposes (such as fundraising). Trudeau determined it would be appropriate to pay **$500** for the brief use of the space.

Jan 10/19 "City News"

The National Energy Board now requires a "Marine Protection Program" prior to pipeline construction. The builder must adhere to the "Canadian Environmental Assessment Act" as well as the Species at Risk Act" Precautions must also be taken to lessen increased underwater noise and potential ship strikes on mammals.

Feb 5/19 "CJ"

Justin Trudeau rejected a Conservative motion from Quebec to transform to a single tax, similar to all other provinces (taxes are submitted to the Federal Government then provincial portions are passed back). Quebec stated it could save $600 million per year but was refused on grounds it would put Canada Revenue people out of work. On Sept 11/19 Ottawa announced funding to construct a new tax centre in Shawinigan Quebec, which will employ 1,500 people.

Mar 2/19 "Times Colonist"

Due to requirements for spill response, which is part of the Trans Mountain Pipeline approval 1 oil skimmer boat and 4 smaller workboats have been delivered and sit idle in Nanaimo British Columbia. The skimmer boat alone is worth $5.8 million and was built in Singapore.

Mar 17/19 CBC News"

Justin Trudeau visited an Ottawa Muslim community and took part in a private meeting to show his solidarity after 50 people were killed in Mosque attacks in Christchurch New Zealand.

Mar 19/19 "National Observer"
The Liberal dominated Justice Committee has put an end to all proceeding of the probe into the SNC-Lavalin affair. Four Liberal MPs submitted resignations over the allegations that Jody Wilson-Raybould was pressured to agree with a "remediation agreement" toward legal charges against the Canadian engineering company. Lisa Raitt accused the Liberal government of controlling witness testimony.

Mar 23/19 "Global News"
Justin Trudeau insists he was trying to protect 9,000 SNC-Lavalin jobs even though the CEO of the company insisted he didn't pressure the government.

Mar 26/19 "CJ"
Canadian citizens Joshua Boyle, Caitlan Coleman and their 3 children born in captivity were rescued from Taliban captivity by Pakistani forces. Upon returning to Canada they were welcomed to a meeting at Parliament hill with Justin Trudeau. This took place 1 week prior to his arrest by Ottawa Police. Boyle is facing charges of assault, sexual assault, unlawful confinement and causing someone to take a noxious substance.

April 9/19 "Global News"
Katherine McKenna announced funding of **$12 million** to Loblaws stores to install more energy-efficient fridges for its retail stores. Loblaws net profit last year after covering interest payments, taxes and other charges was over $800 million. This comes 1 1/2 years after the company fought against the minimum wage, admitted to a 14 year bread price fixing scheme and ended up paying back $368 million in taxes related

to a subsidiary in the Caribbean. The electrical refrigeration units are supposed to be equal to the emissions of 50,000 cars

April 13/19 "CJ"
Hours before Justin Trudeau was to visit Khalsa Diwan society's Gurowara in Vancouver, and then march in Vancouver's Vaisakni parade, wording changes were made to a 2018 public report on terrorism threats to Canada. The Sikh community disliked the wording that "Sikh extremism is one of the top 5 extremist threats to Canada". It will now read as "Threats posed by extremists who support violent means to establish an independent state in India". The Liberal party had 16 Sikh's voted in as MP's in 2015 of which 4 of those are part Trudeau's cabinet.

April 28/19 "CBC News"
According to Statistic Canada the total volume of imported Saudi Arabia oil has risen **66%** over the last 5 years. In 2017 Saudi imports totalled 5.9 million cubic meters worth $2.5 billion. In 2018 imports of Saudi oil increased to 6.4 million cubic meters worth **$3.5 billion.** In 2019 approximately **10%** of Canada's oil consumption will come from Saudi Arabia.

May 4/19 "Frontier Centre"
The Senate Ethics committee is recommending the removal of Senator Lynn Beyak. Originally condemned by Senators and Politicians for making racist comments on her web pages, she has also criticized the Truth and Reconciliation Report as to not being a balanced report. Senator Beyak received hundreds of letters through unsolicited mail from both

Indigenous and non-Indigenous people commending her for her stance. During the political furor Lynn Beyak refused to repent and remove her statements.

May 8/19 "CTV News"
    Canada's Defence Minister Harjit Sajjan regrets what Vice Admiral Mark Norman has gone through over the past years. Government prosecutors stayed the breach of trust charges for leaking cabinet secrets in favour of Quebec based Davies ship Building Company. Davies Shipbuilding was awarded a $700 million Federal contract. Sajjan said he originally agreed with Norman's suspension, therefore would not cover any of the Admiral's court costs, but the situation has now changed. Over 2 years. Norman has amassed over $500,000 in legal fees. General Vance will be talking to Vice-Admiral Norman as to what the next steps will be?

May 10/19 "CJ"
    The Senate Ethics committee has suspended Senator Lynn Beyak without pay for what the Liberal dominated Senate considers racist Indigenous remarks on her website. On her website she made comment that even though there was physical/sexual abuse and death from disease, for many of the children the Residential Schools provided some good.

May 18/19 "CJ"
    Quebec's Davie Shipbuilding has been awarded an advanced contract from the Federal government for the construction of 2 east coast ferries on the pretence that it is the only Canadian shipyard that can meet the construction timeframe. Companies that feel they are capable of this have 15 days to contact the government.

May 19/19 "Express"

Justin Trudeau has been accused of trying to buy media support prior to the next election. A Canadian taxpayer funded **$600 million** commitment has been made toward a newspaper bailout in support of Canadian journalism.

Create a Better Life for Canadians

July 20/16 "CBC News"

The new Child Tax Benefit Program will push 300,000 children out of poverty and help stimulate the economy according to Justin Trudeau. It will be at a cost of **$22.4 billion** over 5 years. A pro-rated system according to income will give families earning less than $30,000 than maximum amount of $6,400 per child per year for each child under the age of 6. They will receive $5,400 per child per year for children between the ages of 6 to 17. Income earners above $200,000 will receive nothing.

Jan 2017 "Canada .ca"

The Federal Contractors Program ensures that contractors that work for the Federal government seek to achieve and maintain a workforce that is representative of the Canadian workforce. As a contractor wishing to bid on Federal contracts worth $1 million after taxes and you maintain a workforce of 100 people you must sign in advance an "Agreement to Implement Employment Equity (LAB 1168). **This agreement specifies you must hire 4 categories of people. Women, Aboriginal people (Indians, Inuit or Metis) Persons with disabilities (long term or reoccurring disabilities) Members of Visible Minorities (people other than Aboriginals and are not Caucasian in race or white in colour)**

Feb 2/17 "Fraser Institute"

In 1917 Ontario Federal workers earned 13.4% more than non-union private sector workers and 10.3% more than unionized workers on average. 82% of Government sector employees have pension plans versus 25% in the private sector. 92% of Government workers belong to a defined benefit pension plan versus 45.1% private sector workers. Federal workers on average retire 1.5 years earlier than private sector employees.

Mar 13/17 "Globe and Mail"

According to Frank Graves, President of the Ekos Research assoc. people self-identifying as middle class has dropped in percentage from **67%** to **46%** of Canada's total population.

Nov 22/17 "Global News"

The Federal government plans to create a "Housing Advocate" and enshrine housing as a human right. A study has been ongoing into a $40 billion National Housing Strategy including personal subsidies is dependant upon the provinces and territories contributing $2 billion. $11.2 billion was outlined in the budget. This will create 60,000 affordable units as well as repairs through grants and loans for coexisting ones.

- For **20 years. 1/3** of all units will be subsidized and offered at **80%** of market value.
- **$4.8 billion** annually will be used to fund affordable housing providers.
- **$100 million** will be contributed toward 3 large scale experiments toward affordable housing models. Other ideas will be tracked but it was stated

that how the money will work is unknown.

- Separate plans are in the works for First Nations Inuit and Metis.

Dec 26/17 "CJ"

A Federal study "Make Poverty Free a Right" presented that Canada's goals should be to reduce poverty nation-wide by 25% over 5 years. This would take into account 840,000 people by 2020 and 2.2 million people in 2030.

Jan 2/18 "CBC News"

Veterans will have to wait until 2019 to choose between a lump sum and a new pension plan introduced by the Federal government. It is clearly a reduction of the lofty scheme Trudeau had personally promised while campaigning. Disability current lump sum payouts is set at a maximum of $360,000 or a tax-free, monthly payment of $1,150/month plus an additional monthly payment of $1500 to those more severely disabled (to which very few will be entitled to). Under the new system a previous supplemental allowance for the most severely disabled will be eliminated. Presently an average monthly payment to spouses is approximately $680/month with a maximum of $2,733 plus added amounts for children. the new payout will be approximately $200/month.

Jan 17/18 "Huffington Post"

Bill Morneau is concerned that the total debt worldwide has hit $240 trillion. Canada's household debt is presently 178 times higher than disposable income.

Mar 2/18 "National Observer"

Justin Trudeau rejected a committee's recommendations to tax foreign online businesses, saying the middle class can't afford another tax. Failing to tax foreign broadcasters such as Netflix is costing the Government over **$1 billion** per year in lost taxes. Netflix bypassed taxes by committing to invest $500 million into Canadian productions over 5 years. The Federal government has provided **$25 million** to Stat's Can. to study and offer a solution to the issue.

June 7/18 "CJ"

Ottawa considers footing the bill to provide housing for homeless veterans. In April 2019 Ottawa plans to launch an emergency fund available for officials to access **$1 million** annually.

July 31/19 "Toronto Sun"

Health care in Canada is not free. Canadians pay a substantial amount for public health care through their taxes. Using data from Statistics Canada and the Canadian Institute for Health Information Taxes are contributed as follows,

- A family of 4 (2 adults - 2 children with a $138,008 annual income contributes **$12,935** toward healthcare
- A couple with an annual income of $57,000 each contributes $12,878
- A single parent with 1 child with an annual income of $60,000 would contribute **$4,357**
- A single Canadian with an annual income less than $60,000 would contribute **$2,115** in 208 but will contribute **$4,460** in 2019
- The 10% of Canadians with an annual income of

$14,885 will contribute **$496**
- The 10% of Canadians with an average annual income $291,364 will contribute **$38,903**

Nov 1/18 "CJ"

In a 850-page budget report the Trudeau government plans to table will give 900,000 people more personal sick leave. This would allow 5 days leave annually, with 3 days of that paid if worker is employed for 3 straight months. Reasons for leave could be, care for relatives, child education, or citizenship ceremonies. They are also looking at an employee being entitled to general holiday pay, sick leave, maternity leave, and parental leave as of day 1 on the job. An additional 5 days paid leave would be for victims of family violence. Unpaid leave for court duty. Entitled to 4 weeks paid annual vacation after working for an employer for 10 consecutive years. An employer would have to provide a written schedule to employees 96 hours prior to the first shift.

Nov 12/18 "CJ"

Prior to electoral defeat the Conservative government predicted a $262.2 billion deficit but a $1.4 billion surplus for 2015-16. The Liberal deficit after 2016-17 was $291.4 billion, an increase of $18.2 billion. The Liberal deficit after 2019-20 is predicted to be $321 billion From 2015 to 2020 the deficit has increased 22%

Nov 25/18 "National Post"

Justin Trudeau was committed improving interprovincial trade by removing trade barriers. He reneged on the commitment by putting blame on the Supreme Court.

Dec 20/18 "CJ"

A new Federal Basic Income Plan in the works will guarantee a minimum income. The Parliamentary Budget Office states that spending will increase to approx. **$43.1 billion** annually, up from the present $32.9 billion. This will provide every Canadian household with a minimum annual income of **$9,431.**

May 6/19 "CBC News"

Child tax benefits will be increased on July 20/19 to **$6,639** for children under the age of 5 years and to **$5,602** for children from the ages of 6 to 17 years. Federal officials state that approximately 1/5 of Indigenous people living on and off Reserves do not collect the benefit. Federal officials will visit **500** rural and remote Reserves to instruct Indigenous people on how to file Income-tax papers. Income tax filing is required prior to being accepted for Child Tax Benefit approval.

Canadian Citizenship and Immigration

Nov 6/16 "Immigration Canada"

Maryam Monsef may be investigated for citizenship fraud after complaints were received from Immigration, Refugees and Citizenship Canada and the Canada Border Services Agency for falsely stating that her birthplace was Afghanistan when it was actually Iran.

Feb 28/17 "CJ"

The Federal government has contributed **$20.3 million** over 5 years. to settle **1,000** refugee women and girls from conflict zones around the world.

Mar 4/17 "Daily Caller"

Amed Hussen the Liberal Immigration Minister introduced Bill C-6 to counter Bill C-24 legislation in parliament because a "Canadian is a Canadian is a Canadian" even if he or she is a convicted terrorist. The

Conservative law Bill C-24 stripped terrorists with dual citizenship of their Canadian status. Hussen said terrorists should go to jail for a long time, but should not include citizenship revocation.

Mar 22/17 "CJ"

A federal House of Commons Committee recommended the government craft a National Antiracism Policy. This is necessary to combat Islamophobia, racism and systematic discrimination. A multiculturalism fund will receive **$23 million** over 2 years toward programs. Stats Canada will receive **$6.7 million** over 5 years to better analyze data, diversity and inclusion.

Aug 18/17 "CBC News"

Refugees entering Canada through Quebec as an example must file a claim with the refugee board, prior to having any access to government or social services they must be:
- Referred to "PRAIDA" a government service that will determine which out of 12 available centres will temporarily house them.
- Declare financial status.
- As a last resort temporary special assistance is available ($628/adult/month) Manitoba assistance is $750/adult /month. Application for a work permit could take up to 4 months. Special assistance ends when the person obtains a job. Access will be available to health services, some prescription drugs and education. Refugees will have the ability to reapply for Canadian status under humanitarian or compassionate grounds if the original application is rejected. Help will be provided to register into

mandatory Federal and Provincial programs.

Aug 31/18 "Toronto Sun"

The Liberal government overturned previous legislation that would strip Canadian Citizenship from dual citizens if convicted of terrorism, treason or espionage. stating a Canadian is a Canadian. Citizenship was reinstated to Amara, a convicted Al-Qaeda ringleader from the Toronto 18 Terrorist cell. Justin Trudeau gave approval to awarding Omar Khadr a **$10.5 million** payout. Another ex- Guantanamo Bay man, Djamel Ameziane with dual citizenship has a $50 million lawsuit pending.

Oct 20/17 "CJ"

The Federal Government is conducting behind closed doors meetings on a new National Anti-racism strategy. Ottawa is consulting experts and participation is by invite only. To date 4 of 24 meetings have taken place.

Jan. 11/18 "CJ"

The Immigration Refugee Board estimates that in 2017 it will require a minimum of $140 million per year to process Immigration claims. Ottawa has pledged a one time **$40 million** to be available to process 36,000 claims per year. The number of outstanding claims has risen to 64,000. Irregular asylum seekers account for **42%** of the backlog.

Feb 12/18 "CBC News"

Jaspal Atwal convicted of attempted murderer of an Indian Cabinet Minister was a former member of an illegal Sikh separatist group was invited to dine with

Prime Minister Justin Trudeau. This was hosted by the Canadian High Commissioner in Delhi India and took place during Canada's trade mission to India.

Feb 16/18 "CJ"

Asylum seekers may wait up to 2 years for refugee claims to be processed. In the 2018 budget the Liberals set aside **$74 million** over 2 years toward the backlog of a projected 60,000 claims. The Federal government is planning to accept an additional 16,500 refugees in 2019 and increase numbers annually up to 20,000 by 2021. Accepted claimants will have instant access to all programs that existing Canadians presently have.

March 1/18 "CJ"

The Federal Government will fund **$25 million** to form a new "anti-racism plan" due to the increase in immigration numbers. A "new centre" will be established to collect and analyze data, on diversity and inclusion and address any immigrant sentiment or racism.

March 3/19 "Capforcanada.com."

The Federal Immigration Minister has initiated the process to restore citizenship to a Convicted terrorist. Amara was put in prison and was as part of the Toronto 18. His citizenship was to be revoked and he was to be deported upon his prison release.

April 11/19 "CJ"

Justin Trudeau defended changes to the asylum laws to ensure Canada's refugee system is fair for everyone. Canada will no longer accept requests from asylum seekers that have previously applied to other countries deemed safe by Canada. This is to end so called "asylum shopping". Out of 41,000 asylum seekers entering Canada in 2017 only 3,100 had previously applied in the United States. Irregular immigrants accounted for 3/4 of all asylum seekers.

April 14/18 "Montreal Gazette"
Montreal is running out of room for border crossers. 2,000 irregular border crossers entered Quebec in 2016, but had increased to 6,074 in 2017. This imposes additional costs to health care and education. The UN estimated the 20,000 of the 50,000 entering Canada in 2017 were irregular.

April 13/18 "CJ"
Data compiled by the Immigration Department shows that immigrant women face more job barriers and earn less than immigrant men and Canadian born women. Canada's immigration minister Ahmed Hussen says the government is working on settlement programs to improve opportunities for immigrant women and children.

April 21/18 "CJ"
Quebec has had a surge of 2,500 kids since 2017 due primarily to asylum seekers.

May 25/18 "CJ"
Canada's Immigration Minister Ahmed Hussen stated the 2018 budget has earmarked $74 million to hire additional Immigrant and Refugee board staff to exclusively process irregular boarder crosser claims, with all cases to be finalized within 12 months. Ahmed

said the main focus will be on quickly processing new files.

June 2/18 "CJ"

Ahmed Hussen says Federal government will contribute funding toward asylum seeker costs to 3 provinces. Quebec will receive **$36 million,** Ontario **$11 million** and Manitoba **$3 million.**

July 9/18 "CTV News"

Immigration Minister Ahmed Hussen announced combined funding to 16 organizations for $113 million. This will be used to connect immigrants to the Canadian job market. These organizations will provide assistance toward job licences, professional qualifications and required skills training.

Aug 3/18 "CJ"

The Federal government's plans to redirect immigrants from Montreal and Toronto to smaller urban centres won't be ready until at least September. Plans would redirect people to other communities while waiting for their claims to be processed. The Federal government presently has contracts with hotels in Mississauga, Etobicoke and Markham to house approx. 500 of the 3,053 asylum seekers living in Toronto.

Aug 16/18 "CJ"

The Federal government has fully restored a program that provides Refugees with temporary health benefits. This came after the United Nations Human Rights committee concluded that Canada violated the rights of an undocumented (illegal) immigrant's access to essential health care. Nell Toussant developed serious health conditions after being denied blood tests and medical procedures due to not having a health card.

Aug 31/18 "Toronto Sun"

The Liberals defeated a Conservative motion to eliminate "birthright citizenship". This was to ensure that one parent had to possess a Canadian Citizenship prior to the newborn becoming a Canadian citizen.

Oct 4/18 "CBC News"

The Canadian Immigration Department changed a web-page about asylum seekers to swap the word "illegal for irregular" This change happened 1 day after Immigration Minister Ahmed Hussen suggested the Provincial Progressive Conservatives were mistaken in the way they were describing the status of people entering Canada at non-official entry points.

Nov. 1/18 "CJ"

Ralph Goodale has asked Canada Border Services to speed up the removal of failed refugee claimants. Additional funding of **$7.46 million** is allocated to remove **10,000** asylum seekers that have exhausted all avenues of appeal. Canada has committed to increasing immigration levels and taking in an additional 40,000 for a total of 350,000 in 2021. They will also increase settlement funding by **30%**. The Federal government plans to increase the number of immigrants under its "Humanitarian Family Reunification and Sponsorship Program" from the current 43,000 to 51,700 people in 2021.

Nov. 16/18 "CJ"

Refugee claims have hit their highest levels since

the start of record keeping 30 years ago. To try and end the backlog an additional 248 staff have been hired for the first nine months of 2018.

Nov. 29/18 "Global News"

According to the Parliamentary Budget Officer Irregular border crossers coming to Canada last year cost the Canadian Government an average of $14,321 in 2017. This covers the entire process of handling their asylum claim. This is expected to rise to $15,483 in 2018 and up to **$16,666** in 2019/20. This could amount to a total of **$340 million** over a 2 to 5 year period. Claims could cost as much as **$33,738** if they go through every appeal process and then have to be deported.

Dec. 26/18 "CJ"

Asylum seekers attempting to cross the border in Manitoba in -35 degree weather in 2016 were granted Canadian Citizenship in 2017. One man lost 10 fingers while the other lost all 10 digits. After years of doctors and rehab, both men are seeking work to pay Canada back. One man is hoping to enrol in a course as a security guard and the other is taking English along with other courses.

Jan 1/19 "www.canada.ca"

Upon arrival to Canada sponsored refugees can apply for Tax free Child Benefits. The Canada Revenue Agency can only make retroactive payments for up to 11 months.

Jan 1/18 "Government of Canada"

The Canadian Charter of Rights protects all

people in Canada. While a refugee claim is being processed people can apply for work permits, student authorization, if minors are involved they have automatic entitlement to education. The Interim Federal Health Program provides limited temporary health care benefits.

Jan. 11/19 "CNN News"

Immigration Refugees and Citizenship has pledged **$5.6 million** to support "Global Resettlement Initiatives" The Federal government plans to help more than one million new immigrants in the next 3 years.

Jan 15/19 "CJ"

Chrystia Freeland officially welcomed Rahaf al-Qunun as a Canadian citizen. Rahaf gained global attention by her plight to escape from family in Saudi Arabia. She fled her family while visiting Kuwait, flew to Bangkok and barricaded herself into an airport hotel, where she launched a twitter account alleging parental abuse. Rahaf publicly stated that she wished to seek asylum in Canada or Australia. Justin Trudeau stated she would be welcome in Canada, then later said Rahaf would be accepted at a UN request. Since becoming a Canadian citizen Rahaf's priorities are to access a health card, get a bank account, get a phone and update her wardrobe for Canada's climate.

Jan 19/19 "capforcanada.com"

Convicted terrorist Tahawwur Hussain Rana a dual Pakistani/Canadian citizen will be allowed back in Canada. He is one of 10 terrorists that the previous Harper Government had stripped of Citizenship. Bill C-6 contains new legislation that will restore Canadian

Citizenship to convicted terrorists.

Jan 24/19 "CBC News"

Communities have until March 30 to submit proposals to be in the lottery for funding opportunities to bring skilled immigrants to their communities. Under the Canadian Charter of Rights people cannot be forced or expected to stay in any given location.

Jan. 25/19 "CJ"

A new "Rural Pilot Program" will be implemented to try to have skilled immigrant workers and families relocate to smaller communities. Towns with populations under 50,000 people can submit proposals to take in immigrants. Bids submitted must prove there is settlement infrastructure available, language and employment support services. The process is open to all provinces except Quebec and the Atlantic provinces. The program is available for up to 3,000 immigrants with a maximum of 100 skilled people and their families per community. Successful communities will be notified by spring.

Jan 30/19 "CJ"

Ottawa announces an additional **$114 million toward housing asylum seekers over and above to $50 million** already allowed to Quebec, Ontario and Manitoba.

Feb. 2/19 "CJ"

Appearing at a town hall meeting in Mirimichi, New Brunswick Justin Trudeau reminded the people that it was his government that brought in 40,000 Syrian refugees in 2015-16. Trudeau accused the

Conservatives of "fear mongering over immigrants" after he was questioned about signing a UN agreement "Global Compact for Safe Orderly and Regular Migration.

Feb. 2/19 "CJ"
Andrew Scheer criticized Justin Trudeau's tweet in 2017 welcoming all people fleeing persecution, terror or war. Federal records show that 34,854 claims were made from irregular border crossers. From Feb 2017 to Sept 2018, 3,142 have been accepted (equal to 9%)

Feb 22/19 "CJ"
Justin Trudeau attended a Vigil in Halifax for 7 children killed in a house fire. The family immigrated to Canada approximately one year ago.   Immediate priority has been given by the minister of immigration to grant instant Canadian citizenship for 5 to 10 relatives of the surviving parents.

Mar 20/19 "CJ"
The pre-election budget plans to spend **$1.8 billion** over 5 years to toughen border security and hire additional judges to review asylum applications.

Mar 21/19 "CJ"
Asylum seeker Vanessa Rodel and her 7-year-old daughter were granted asylum to Canada. Vanessa was part of the group that sheltered whistleblower Edward Snowden. She has since pleaded with the government to allow others that assisted to also gain asylum. Money has been collected towards costs by people in Canada.

Mar 28/19 "CJ"

The Liberal 2019 budget committed to boost funding for Canada's Refugee Health Program by **$183 million** over 2 years. This is required due to more people making refugee claims. Health care is Canada's valued humanitarian tradition. Ensuring the most vulnerable people has access to basic health care.

May 16 "CJ"

Citizenship ceremonies took place in Thunder Bay for 80 new Canadian's. To obtain citizenship these people had to meet requirements. The applicants had to spend 1,095 days or a minimum of 3 of the last 5 years in Canada. Everyone was required to pass a citizenship test, demonstrate a certain competency in either French or English, file income tax, and have no criminal record.

May 18/19 "CJ"

The Liberal government has eliminated the "safe country policy" created by the former Conservative government. This policy divided refugee claimants into categories to deter abuse of the system. Refugees from 42 countries deemed as being safe were put through an expedited process. In 2016 - 16,000 asylum seekers made claims in Canada. Two years later in 2017 there were 50,000 and in 2018 there were 55,000 refugee applicants. Statistics Canada shows that the greater number of asylum seekers are male and younger than Canada's general population.

May 26/19 "Global News"

The United Nations is urging Canada to take more Central America migrants to ease Mexico's refugee burden. Asking that Canada take some of the most vulnerable including women, children and LGBTQ2 persons. People from Honduras, El Salvador and Venezuela have spiked refugee claims in Mexico by 103% to 30,000 claims. Women and girls fleeing gang violence, transgender and gay people should be resettled in a country where they would consider to be safe. Canada's Immigration minister was unable to provide statistics as to the number of Mexican asylum seekers Canada has received recently. Canada is a partner in the Rainbow Refugee Society which helps sponsor LGBTQ2 refugees from around the world. This year Canada has sponsored 64 refugees.

Gender Equality

April 18/16 "Canadian Centre For Policy Alternatives"
This organization states the average pay gap between men and women is 29.4%

Oct 27/16 "CJ"
A newly created government agency "Status of Women Canada" will receive **$41 million** in 2016, **$4 million** in 2017 and **$8 million** per year consecutive for 5 years. to focus on gender equality.

Feb 28/17 "CJ"
In the new budget "Status of Women" will receive an additional **$100 million** over 5 years. toward gender equality.

Feb 28/17 "CJ"
The Federal government is implementing measures to boost the number of women entrepreneurs with a **$1.4 billion** commitment over 3 years from the Business Development bank.
- Commit **$105 million** over 5 years. to fund Regional Development Agencies that support women led businesses.
- Start a Pilot Apprenticeship Grant of **$19.9** million which will provide up to $6,000 per person for women entering male dominated skilled trades.
- Stats. Canada will receive **$67 million** over 5 years. and an additional $600,000 per year after to set up

    a new Centre for Gender, diversity and inclusion statistics.

- Contribute **$1.8 million** over 2 years. to develop a strategy to help men and boys better understand gender equality.
- Funding of **$5.5 million** over 5 years will be used to develop a national frame-work aimed at addressing gender based violence in colleges and universities.
- The federal "Gender-Based Violence Strategy" will receive **$86 million** over 5 years. to focus on preventing dating violence among teenagers and will also be used to support "Sexual Assault Centres" located near Canadian Forces Bases.

Feb 28/17 "CJ"

    The Federal government will spend **$39.4 million** over 5 years and an additional **$7.4 million** annually to support proposed legislation to crack down on harassment in federally regulated work places.

Feb 28/17 "CJ"

    Ottawa's "Feminist International Development Policy" Has committed **$2 billion** over 5 years to focus on supporting girls around the world.

Mar 1/17 "CJ"

    The Federal Government is contributing **$30 million** over 3 years to produce data and research to understand why fewer women and girls take part in sports and other physical activities than men and boys. This will help show why less women advance to senior levels of coaching and management.

April 26/17 and June 19/17 "CJ"

Federal Judge Martine St Lois approved a compensation package for military and other government services worth between **$50 and $100 million.** People discriminated or fired due to their sexual orientation as early as 1940 will be eligible to receive between **$5,000 and $175,000** depending on the severity of the case. It is estimated as many as 1,000 people may be part of the class action lawsuit. An Exceptions Committee will be created for a case by case review. A monument is to be erected in the Museum of Human Rights.

Jan 25/18 "CBC News"

While participating in a panel discussion on "the "empowerment of Women and girls" at the World Economic Forum in Switzerland Justin Trudeau committed to **$180 million** over 3 years. This will double its commitment in aid for girls education to the Global Partnership for Education fund.

June 9/18 "BBC News"

At the Quebec based G-7 Summit Justin Trudeau pledged **$2.9 billion** (with a request for help from other G-7 countries) to educate the world's poorest women and girls.

Sept 23/18 "CJ"

Ottawa is to name an Ambassador to Women, dedicated to peace and security of women. This person will champion feminine based aid programs and advocate for more female participants in peacekeeping and conflict resolutions. Ottawa has generated a fund of **$25 million** for initiatives to combat gender based violence.

Nov 25/18 "CBC News"
The Federal Government is contributing **$450,000** to Toronto for LGTBQ safety.

Dec 4/18 "CJ"
Ottawa will contribute **$20 million** to the global charity "Education Cannot Wait", which educates children affected by poverty, natural disasters and other crisis. This has been earmarked to educate women and girls around the world.

Jan 1/19 "City News"
According to the "Canadian centre For Policy Alternatives" gender pay gap is widest to the top of the corporate ladder. Women on average earn $0.68 for every $1.00 men make.

April 13/19 "CJ"
A House of Commons Committee is calling for the Federal Government to offer cash incentives to Political parties that nominate more women candidates to run for election.

Indigenous Relations

2016 Federal Budget
(A Better Future For Indigenous People)

A total investment that exceeds the negotiated sum of the Kelowna Accord, this budget represents a 22% increase to Indigenous funding $8.4 billion allocated over 5 years (table rounded out to the nearest million dollars)

	2016	2017	2018	2019	2020
EDUCATION to ensure reserve and non-reserve are comparable. $2.6 billion over 5 years					
On Reserve infrastructure	$194	$194	$194		
Skills/training strategy	$7.5	$7.5			
Address immediate needs and cost growth	$36	$86	$144	$206	$276
Implement transformation	$47	$91	$133	$243	$319
Literacy/Numeracy	$20	$20	$20	$20	$20
Special needs	$116	$116	$116	$116	$116
Early learning/child care	$29	$100			
Better learning environment	$97	$283	$197	$184	$209
Improve how reading and writing is taught	$6	$6	$6	$6	$6
Administrative costs	$1	$2	$2	$2	$2
Language/culture support	$55	$55	$55	$55	$55

	2016	2017	2018	2019	2020
Innovation research and evaluation	$6	$6	$6	$6	$6
Preserve/promote/enhance Aboriginal language	$5	$5	$5	$5	$5

Social Infrastructure
$1.2 Billion over 5 years

	2016	2017	2018	2019	2020
Family/child services	$73	$73	$73	$73	$73
Immediate housing needs	$206	$206			
Canada Mortgage and Housing renovations	$69	$69			
Housing for women and children fleeing violence	$3	$3	$3	$3	$3
Victims of violence	$7	$7	$7		
Affordable child care/head start on-reserve program	$29				
Affordable housing, Yukon, NW, Nunavut, Nunavik, Nunatasluvat and Inuvialuit	$89	$89			
Health care offices and worker residences	$54	$54	$54	$54	$54
Cultural and recreational infrastructure	$30	$30			
First Nations infrastructure (roads, energy, broadband)	$112	$112			

	2016	2017	2018	2019	2020

Green Infrastructure
$2.2 billion over 5 years

	2016	2017	2018	2019	2020
Operation and maintenance of water and wastewater	$36	$36	$36	$36	$36
Water Testing 141.7 million over 5 years	$27	$27	$55		
Divert garbage from reserve land, recycle and compost	$82	$82	$82	$82	$82

Justice

Missing and Murdered Aboriginal Women inquiry	$20	$20			
Organizations in spirit of cooperation with the government 96 million over 5 years plus 10 million ongoing	$19	$19	$19	$19	$19
Indigenous engagement	$16	$20			
Other Initiatives	$217	$202	$44	$46	$47
Advise Indigenous people of their rights in court	$5	$5	$5	$5	$5
Fund First Nations Finance Authority toward investments	$10	$10			

Off-Reserve Funding

Metis Nation Economic Development	$5	$5	$5	$5	$5

	2016	2017	2018	2019	2020
Urban Aboriginal Study assistance for urban relocation	$51	$51	$51	$51	$51
Costs associated with challenging Historical grievances, lost lands and mishandled Trust Funds	$24	$24	$24	$24	$24

2017 Federal Budget
(Setting a Path For Reconciliation)

$3.4 billion commitment over and above the $8.4 billion commitment in the 2016 budget (table rounded to nearest million dollars).

	2017	2018	2019	2020
Education				
Protect and promote Indigenous language	$30	$30	$30	
Improve primary and secondary education	$288	$283		
First Nation post-secondary	$900			
Post-secondary student support	$45	$45		
Indigenous students pursuing College or University (approximately 12,000)	$40			
Better learning environment	$97	$283		
Adult basic education	$5	$5	$5	
Skills/employment strategy	$50			
Costs associated with challenging historical grievances, lost lands and mishandled Trust Funds	$24	$24	$24	$24

Social Infrastructure
$1.5 billion over 5 years.

	2017	2018	2019	2020
Improve First Nation housing	$277	$277		
Improve Northern/Inuit housing	$277	$277		
Safe houses/shelters for victims of violence	$5	$5		
Culture and recreation	$35	$42		
Indigenous tourism industry	$2	$2	$2	$2
Support for Indigenous fisheries	$250			
Non-insured health benefits	$61	$61	$61	$61
Access to mental health services	$18	$17	$17	$17
Mental health programming	$24	$24	$24	$24
Mental health support and traditional healers	$41	$41	$41	
Home and palliative care	$37	$37	$37	$37
Primary care	$14	$14	$14	$14
Chronic and infectious disease	$10	$10	$10	$10
Drug reduction strategy	$3	$3	$3	$3
Allow expectant mothers to Bring a partner				
Expand maternal and child care for children under 7 years.	$17	$17	$17	$17
Safety and wellbeing of First Nations children	$24	$24	$24	$24

	2017	2018	2019	2020
Early child care support	$29	$100		

Justice

	2017	2018	2019	2020
Promote "restorative justice"	$11			
Rehabilitate/reinstate criminal offenders	$13			
First Nation Police services	$16			
Fund a Secretariat to support a "working group" regarding Indigenous laws and policies	$1	$1	$1	
Case management for On-Reserve youth	$39			

Off-Reserve Funding

Northern and Off-Reserve housing (over 11 years)	$27	$27	$27	$27
Funding for Off-Reserve housing partners	$20	$20	$20	$20
Fund Off-Reserve Native Friendship Centres	$24	$24	$24	$24

2018 Federal Budget (Plus Reconciliation)

$5 billion has been committed over and above the combined $11.8 billion 2016 and 2017 commitment. This is to ensure Indigenous women and families have an equal chance to succeed in life. $2 billion over 5 years will be funded for Aboriginal skills development. $1.1 billion over 5 years will be funded to implement a new "Stream Program" designed with a distinction based approach that recognizes the unique needs for Indigenous people to develop the skills required for higher paying jobs.

(table rounded to the nearest million dollars)

	2018	2019	2020	2021
Education				
First Nations "Stream Program"	$2,200	$2,200	$2,200	$2,200
Inuit "Stream Program"	$32	$32	$32	$32
Create a new Indigenous "Skills Program"	$408	$408	$408	$408
Focus put on higher paying jobs rather than rapid re-employment (assist approx. 15,000 people)	$89	$89	$89	$89
Strengthen Indigenous data and research capability	$4	$1	$1	$1
Funds to Match Gord Downie, Chanie, Wenjack Fund (teaching about Residential Schools)	$5			

	2018	2019	2020	2021
Social Infrastructure				
Ensure Indigenous children are safe in their communities.	$70	$295	$270	$265
On-Reserve housing	$200	$200	$200	$200
Inuit housing "Plan Program will commit $400 million over 10 years	$40	$40	$40	
Capacity building in First Nation communities	$47	$47	$47	$47
Funding to support "Indigenous Self-Government"	$189			
Funding toward Indigenous "Rights and Self Determination"	$320	$148	$49	$49

Health
$1.5 billion over 5 years

	2018	2019	2020	2021
Increase health support for Residential School Survivors	$73	$83	$88	
24-7 Nursing Stations in 79 remote communities.	$496			
Addictions treatment	$40	$40	$40	$40
Develop a Health System controlled by First Nations	$235			
Non-insured health benefits	$245	$245		

	2018	2019	2020	2021
Inuit communities with high rates of Tuberculosis 109 million over 10 years.	$11	$11	$11	$11
Access to critical care	$100	$100	$100	$100
Support Inuit health priorities	$14	$14	$14	$14

Off-Reserve Funding

	2018	2019	2020	2021
Metis "Stream Program" $65 million over 5 years	$213	$65	$64	$65

Urban non-affiliated "Stream Program" $213 million over 5 years	$43	$43	$43	$43
Metis Nation housing $500 million over 5 years	$50	$50	$50	$50
Metis Nation post-secondary education	$10			
Metis Nation priorities	$10			
Metis Nation health data collection	$1	$1	$1	$1
Metis Nation health strategy	$1	$1	$1	$1

Crown Indigenous Relations and Northern Affairs Canada Planned 2018-19 Budget

CIRNAC controls funding over treaty rights and land negotiations CIRNAC is committed to becoming the employer's choice of Indigenous people (2018-19 year end Mar 31)

Operating budget $3.086 billion. (3108 full-time employees)

Breakdown
- Internal Services: $206,679 million (1,231 full-time employees)
- Rights and Self Determination: $2.233 billion (1,021 full-time employees)
- Community and Regional Development: $646.678 million (856 full time employees)

Amount of money not allocated to Core Responsibilities
- 2016-17 $6.4 million
- 2017-18 $4 million
- 2018-19 Not Available

Indigenous Services Canada

ISC Controls funding over Indigenous health care, water and services. ISC is committed to become the employer of choice for Indigenous people

Dec 20/18 "Frontier Centre"
Indigenous Services and Crown Indigenous Relations, no matter how they are divided maintains jurisdiction over 90% of Canada's land mass, through historic and modern treaties (signed after 1975). Indigenous Affairs (IA) is a federally funded entity. Provinces and Territories as well are funded federally but those monetary numbers are published. Prior to 2004-05 IA published the names and contributors of the co-delivery partners, after that they no longer did. During 2005-06 IA's funding was $5.8 billion plus an additional $3 billion for 13 co-delivery partners. A total of $8.8 billion toward services and programs, IA had a 2017-18 budget of $10 billion, but according to Indian Affairs there were 33 additional co-delivery partners (Federal agencies and departments) for Indigenous programs and services. An estimate of the total budget would be $19 billion. If these figures showed as transfer payments IA would be 3rd in line monetarily, behind Quebec at $22.7 billion and Ontario at $21.1 billion. 4th would be British Columbia at $6.7 billion. Ottawa has pledged an additional $4.2 billion over 5 years as well as an additional $1.7 billion over 10 years. Indigenous Affairs has jurisdiction over the majority of the 1.5

million people who self-identify as Indigenous. A normal Federal Department has the elected PM appoints the Minister, who is accountable to the PM and Cabinet. The Minister then appoints Department heads. IA has power over First Nations and Inuit from birth to death yet not a single Indigenous Affairs person is elected to any position by ordinary Indigenous people. If this was to take place in the Provinces, it would be considered an outrage to democracy.

Indigenous Services Canada
2018 Operating Budget: $9.485 billion
(696 full time employees)

Breakdown

- First Nations and Inuit Health: $3.092 billion (1985 full-time employees)
- Well Being of Individuals and Families: $4.343 billion. (496 full-time employees)
- Community and Regional Development: $1,825 billion (66 full-time employees)

Indigenous Reconciliation

Mar 4/17 "CJ"
The majority Northern Ontario First Nations are about to receive a significant portion of the **$100 million** from stumpage fees and mining taxes. Grand Council Treaty 3 (Wan tribal council and Mushkegowuk council will receive **45%** of stumpage fees and **40%** of mining taxes and royalties where-ever this takes place on "traditional land." Tribes will have full control of monies collected.

Mar 7/22 "CJ"
The Federal government prepares for consultation to combat racism. Should all Canadians be responsible for what took place in the creation of residential schools?

July 27/17 "CJ"
Indigenous artwork is to be installed (available for sale) in the Thunder Bay Regional Hospital. This is to enhance the hospitals welcoming environment to Indigenous peoples. Sensitivity training in "Ojibwa" languages will be made available to staff and volunteers. (It is noted that a similar program towards native art has taken place in the Toronto General Hospital.)

May 7/17 "CJ"
Five hundred members of the Lheidli Tenneh First Nation in BC will receive 43 square kilometres of

land and $37 million plus ongoing funding for health care, education and social development.

June 30/17 "The Star"

Justin Trudeau visited Indigenous activists the set up on Parliament Hill. RCMP had initially resisted the efforts of the activists setting up teepees ahead of Saturday's Canada Day Celebrations.

Sept 18/17 "Frontier Centre"

The Indian Act says that Status Indians living on reserves should be treated as children and important decisions for them should be made by others. The main reason to possess a Status Card is to allow you special financial benefits not available to others. The 2 main examples are tax exemptions and post-secondary education benefits. An Indigenous person earning a six-figure income, paying no income tax, can also have their children's college or university education and expenses paid in full. Mainstream Canadians have none of these privileges. These entitlements are allowed but abused by off-reserve middle-class Status people. The on-reserve people with low-paying jobs or collecting welfare cannot benefit from these same exemptions. The numbers of on-reserve children attending post-secondary educations is also less than off-reserve Indigenous youth.

Nov 2/17 & Nov 27/17 "Frontier Centre"

The history of Residential schools is now being taught to children in all schools. Most noticeable is the case of Chanie Wenjack. He is portrayed as an unhappy Indigenous boy who ran away from a Residential school after suffering sexual and physical abuse from Roman

Catholic Priests. The Truth and Reconciliation report showed no reliable evidence to support this even though it has reported in books, CBC videos, a song and media articles. Gord Downie's book "Secret Path" is probably the most publicized, showing Native children sitting at desks, overseen by Catholic priests and nuns (in standard Catholic collars and habits). Chanie was actually boarded at the Cecellia Jeffery Residence in Kenora along with 150 others. This at one time was a Residential school run by Presbyterians. Colin Wasacase, of the Saultaux Cree, was the hostel's administrator and his wife was the Matron. This typifies the misleading information. Many of the supervisors as well were Indigenous. The truth and Reconciliation Report quietly notes that many of the sexual predators in the Residential schools were actually older students preying on the younger ones. As an example of the good was the Assininaboia Residential school in Manitoba. It produced an Indigenous hockey team from which 8 of the players went on to become Chiefs in their communities. Another was Tomson Highway, a novelist and playwright who talks about the good as well as the bad. Gord Downie's book "Secret Path" is presently being used as a teaching aid in 40,000 classrooms across Canada. Entire generations will grow up to teachings that have little credible information.

Nov 17/17 "CJ"

Indigenous Services Minister Jane Philpott calls an emergency meeting on Indigenous child welfare. The "Human Rights Tribunal" says Indigenous children are still being taken and put into the welfare system at an alarming rate. (Harry Belegarde is asking for **$155 million** to find out why)

Nov 25/17 "CJ"

Justin Trudeau apologizes to Newfoundland's Residential School–survivors. Newfoundland was not included in the $50 million settlement due to the province not joining Confederation until 1947, therefore they were still under British rule.

Dec 4/17 "Frontier Centre"

There has been a rise and this will continue to accelerate in the number of people claiming status. A Status card allows special rights other Canadians are not entitled to. These benefits can include a complete income tax exemption if a person lives on a reserve and works elsewhere, or a person that works on a reserve and lives elsewhere. An example is that if an Indigenous institution has its main office on reserve land, but maintains sub offices in areas off of reserve land the Indigenous employees are not required to pay income tax. Status gives the children the right to free post-secondary education benefits including grants to pay for books, room and board. Simply put, a high salaried Status Indigenous person may not have to pay income tax or sales tax and will receive free education for their children paid for by the taxpayer. When the Indian Act was legislated in 1876 it created a dependence on the government and financial benefits were continually added. Indigenous status numbers have increased due partially to birthrate.

In 2017 legislation was passed to end sexual discrimination thus amending the Indian Act and allow women prior to 1982 that married white men the right to regain their status rights. This also allowed the right to pass status onto children if the mother died prior to

1985, similar to the male rights. The "Daniels Case" has the possibility of allowing hundreds of thousands of Metis people to also gain status entitlements. Government records show that between 2006 and 2016 the "self-identified Indigenous population" grew by **42.5%** making it **1,673,785** people. Metis numbers grew by **51%** to **587,545** people. Non status Indigenous people grew by **75.1%**. The large majority of Indigenous people do not live on reserves. The Manitoba Metis President David Chartrand expressed concern that people are seeking Metis status primarily for financial benefit, defeating the objective of righting past wrongs. These very expensive supplemental benefits are causing a divide in the country. Mainstream Canadians earning in many cases lower incomes are not entitled to benefits that higher income Indigenous people may receive. Many of the off-reserve status people are descendants of people that previously left reserves seeking a better life. It is these people who stand to gain the most compared to the low income or unemployed people on reserves.

In 1876 Sir John A. Macdonald gave people the choice; they could isolate themselves on reserves or become enfranchised. This meant the people would be compensated for lost rights but from that point on would have the same status as all other Canadians. A Federal government shows that despite the massive increases in funding since 1981 there has been no appreciable improvement for on-reserve residents as far as far as housing, drug and alcohol dependency, teenage pregnancies or suicides. The wealthy are becoming wealthier with the present system.

Dec 7/17 "CJ"

Canada's Parliamentary watchdog says changes to the Indian Act will eliminate sexism by reinstating Women's Indigenous status rights. Prior to 1985 Native women who married white males lost their status, therefore not being able to pass on these rights to their children. Up to 67,000 people could be eligible to claim status. Estimated costs would be **$71 million** for administrative costs plus an additional **$407 million** per year in continuing costs. Annual costs may vary by the number of people planning for relocate to Reserves. All recipients will receive full Treaty Rights.

Dec 7/17 "CJ"

Letter to Editor - Neither Chanie Wenjack nor his sisters attended Residential schools. The actual school attended was a public schooling Kenora Ontario started by a Presbyterian Women's Mission. Neither priests nor nun's taught there. Chanie died while trying to return home walking along a railway line in the winter. Stated at an inquest by a best friend of Chanie was lonely and wanted to return home. The book by Gord Downie was lacking facts.

Dec 17/17 "CJ"

The "Indigenous Stream of the Ontario Local Poverty Reduction Fund "will contribute **$5.3 Million** to 14 programs that work to obtain low-income Indigenous families gain identification. Many Indigenous families are not able to collect child care benefits due to the birth of children not being registered. Last year the Kinna-Aweya Legal Clinic accessed approx. $1.2 million in benefits to people it represented.

Jan 5/18 "Frontier Centre"

Senator Lynn Beyak was removed from Cabinet for saying what many people think is true. She had the audacity to suggest that Residential Schools had done some good. Without them, connections to the modern world would have otherwise been unavailable to Indigenous children. Many Indigenous high school graduates still have trouble with wage labour due to hunting and gathering life ways, dependency on government transfers and royalties for their substance. The activists that chastised Beyak are educated and live comfortably in urban environments. It is these people that abuse the settler guilt about atrocities by their colonizing ancestors. Perceived racism has made it impossible to hold an open discussion between Indigenous and Non-Indigenous people. Activists with a modern education control the debates and it is these activists that are determined to have their people return to a lifestyle of the past.

Jan 8/18 "Frontier Centre"

In 2013 the parliament passed the "First Nations Financial Transparency Act" This made it law that First Nations Chiefs and band council's salaries, and audited statements be made public—something the rest of Canadians take for granted. Enforcement of the "FNFTA" ended in 2015 with Justin Trudeau's elected majority. Prior to cancellation, Native Bands were **90%** compliant. Today the Bands are **80%** compliant.

Frontier Centres Aboriginal Index, with a mostly Indigenous Staff testified after surveying 1,000 people from 100 communities that 77% of the people felt transparency was needed. An Ottawa think tank said transparency was essential for attracting outside investment.

Feb 20/18 "Frontier Centre"

A class-action lawsuit has been filed against the Federal Government over a claim by an Indigenous female patient that she was abused at an Indian Hospital in the 1960s when she was 10 years old.

Feb 24/18 "Frontier Centre"

Native activists and Chiefs were quick at putting blame when Colten Boushie was shot. What about the farmers and townspeople living close to reserves? The five people that entered Gerald Stanley's property obtained no criminal charges. The group jumped into a pick-up Stanley was fixing, tried to start an ATV and drove a Ford Escape into Stanley's wife's vehicle. One of the 5 stated he had consumed 30 shots of alcohol. Boushie's blood alcohol was 4 times the driving limit without any charges being laid. Is Justin Trudeau and the Justice Minister telling us there are 2 sets of rules? This was a home invasion that happened in broad daylight.

April 29/18 "Frontier Centre"

The Truth and Reconciliation Report recommended that sanctions should address that people are on treaty land. In a CBC interview with a person describing himself as a "treaty official" said that when new immigrants come to Canada he explains that Canada is in fact treaty land and they are expected to honour the treaties and share the land, (with the exception to reserve lands are described in the Indian Act) Other lands were compensated for. Indigenous elite are obtaining expensive lawyers in a "Share the Land" marketing campaign. They wish to have treaties rewritten rather than interpreted. This would force present land owners share their land. New treaties will only make the privileged few richer yet not solve the chronic poverty and unemployment on reserves.

Mar 2/18 "CJ"
　　Alberta wraps up '60s Scoop Apology. An estimated **20 to 25 thousand** Indigenous children were taken from their homes from 1951 to 1991.

Mar 8/18 "CJ"
　　Too many Reserves have what is called normalized abuse. Inuit women should take back control. Sex offenders should be banished from Inuit communities. Abuse on Reserves is not an Inuit problem; it is from colonialism and ideologies.

Mar 18/18 Frontier "Centre"
　　The Ontario Medical Association recently voted down a motion to open its meetings with the acknowledgment "You are on Treaty Land"

May 5/18 "CJ"
　　Newly formed Missenabe Cree First Nation was created 112 years after the band demanded its own land base. Left out of the James Bay Treaty of 1906, the 500-member Band northeast of Wawa Ontario will receive 40,000 sq. kilometres, complete with rights to natural resources.

May 18/18 "Frontier Centre"
　　From the 1950s to the 1980s thousands of

Aboriginal and Metis children were apprehended and placed in non-Aboriginal care. An estimated **20,000** Indigenous '60s Scoop survivors will receive compensation of **$75 million** with an additional **$50 million** toward a Foundation. Lawyers' fees of **$75 Million** were also charged, for a total of **$875 million.**

June 1/18 "Frontier Centre"

Bill C-69 brought in by the Liberal government will require "Indigenous Traditional Knowledge" on environmental assessments, even though there is no actual definition to what traditional knowledge is? According to a CBC radio interviews stated Traditional Knowledge is the same as Indigenous science. This is knowledge passed through generations such as animal movement for hunters, changes in weather and plant-based medicine. The bill also makes it illegal to force anyone with possession of Traditional Knowledge to divulge it without the keeper's written consent. A keeper is (in plain definition) "a Medicine Man." Traditional knowledge is no more than religious beliefs being imposed upon proven modern science.

June 2/18 "CJ"

Indigenous '60s Scoop survivors need no proof of suffering or harm done. A prime factor that caused removal of many of the Aboriginal children was Fetal Alcohol Syndrome.

June 5/18 "Frontier Centre"

Indigenous people of today feel that their rights are absolute and overrule everything else. This showed when Saskatchewan based Federation of Sovereign Nations Chef Bobby Cameron stated it was his right to be able hunt on any pasture land without requiring the owners/farmers permission. The Supreme Court ruled that safety overruled what they thought were Indigenous rights.

June 7/18 "Frontier Centre"

Prior to abduction from families and placing children as temporary wards to the Crown proof as to why the children should be removed was required. After that additional proof was required showing that there were no possible options for placement back to parents, relatives or siblings (usually due to safety). These children were then made permanent wards of the crown. The cause of the '60s Scoop rests on booze. Booze was the destroyer of marriages, families, relationships, jobs and support. It was booze that scooped up these children and dumped them into foster homes.

July 28/18 "CJ"

John A. Macdonald statue was removed from Victoria City Hall. This was a gesture of Reconciliation due him being a key architect in the creation of the residential school system.

July 28/18 "CJ"

A lawsuit representing dozens of descendants of Inuit people forced into relocation has been settled for **$5 million** by the federal government. In the 1950s due to construction of a Canadian Army radio station in Arviat, Nunavut people were forcefully relocated from their traditional land leaving many to starve.

Aug 2/18 "Frontier Centre"

Metis are descendants of Indigenous women and

white men. They began amalgamating as a distinct people by taking control of territory controlled by Indigenous tribes (mostly Ojibway), yet they use the phrase "you're on my home land". The Ojibway tribe, which originated from what is now western Ontario and took control from enemy tribes such as the Woodland Cree for hunting territory in Manitoba. There was constant back and forth possession with the Lakota Tribe that was taught horsemanship from the Spanish. Mohawks displaced the Hurons through mass slaughter. Every Tribe would have to claim they are on someone else land possibly dating as far back to the Siberian ancestors.

Aug 18/18 "Frontier Centre"

An estimated **100,000** "Day school survivors could be paid out as much as **$5 billion**. The lawsuit stems from being forced to learn English, subject to discipline, and not allowed to speak their language. From the 1950s discipline was common in all schools. The step or caring was a common discipline to all school attendee's no matter ethnic culture or racial background. Forcing Native children to learn English rather than teaching 60 Native dialects was a way of allowing children to have a better chance of succeeding in a modern world. Amounts paid out as Reconciliation Residential School Survivors - per person $10,000 per year in attendance, damaged children receive more. '60s Scoop per person $35,000 without having to prove anything. Payments to people who were rescued and placed in better homes were paid as well. Missing and Murdered Aboriginal Women and Girls that fled for their own protection may be entitled to the next taxpayer pay-out.

Aug 22/18 "Frontier Centre"

The average Canadian knows that 86 Residential schools existed from 1960 to 1996. Today's media focusses mainly on the more sensational aspects such as helpless, tormented, physically and sexually abused youth, removed from culture and being torn from their parents arms by Indian Agents or RCMP. No one is trying to hide the fact that there was cultural repression, abuse, forced incarceration or even preventable deaths. The system should have done more but facts show frequency was less than the media states. It is easier for the Canadian public to blame all present issues on past practice. Enrolment figures show that the Residential schools had a **10% to 15%** absentee rate. The 253 Day Schools operating up to 1950 had a **50%** absentee rate. After funding was secured the absentee rate dropped to the **20% to 30%** range.

Sept 11/17 "Frontier Centre"

When changes were made to the Indigenous and Northern Affairs Canada, it was to establish an Indigenous Relations / Negotiations Department until they become self-sufficient. How will we know if they are self-sufficient when the transparency act was abolished? The Act was meant to show Chiefs salaries as well as revenue received over and above Federal Transfer payments.

Sept 13/18 "Frontier Centre"

Action #14 of the Truth and Reconciliation Recommendations calls for the teaching of Indigenous languages in public schools to be a priority. Teaching of 60 different Indigenous languages in schools would maintain little future accomplishment and fluency with people learning these languages so few, and so spread out. Latin was also a once used language. Pride, culture and history are important but to take time in schools away from teaching the basics (i.e. math, English and science) would not be productive. Teaching of Ancestral languages should be something best done by parents, community groups and ethnic associations. The government should be committed to providing the best possible education for all Canadians. With Canada being a multicultural country of all races and nationalities, they too would like to be accommodated in the same way.

Sept 17/18 "National Post"

Ken Hill, a 59 year-old businessman and a member of 6 Nations Reserve in Branford Ontario in 1992 co-founded "Grand River Enterprises Ltd" which takes in over $300 Million in global cigarette sales annually. Ken does not pay taxes due to Indian Act exemptions. Due to a divorce a court disclosure showed Ken making a $45.49 Million salary per year. He owns a $1.135 million home in Kitchener Ontario, 7 sports cars valued at $5.58 Million, a 76 foot yacht worth $2.76 Million, a Searay Sundancer boat valued at $939 thousand and joint interest in a 10 seater plane.

Sept 21/18 "Frontier Centre"

When the Robinson Treaty was signed, compensation was paid and land reserved but hunting and fishing would still be allowed on surrendered land. The people would continue to provide for their own needs on their reserves. When treaties were signed there were no such things as welfare cheques or transfer payments. The Federal government now spends approx. **$100,000** per year on each First Nation family.

Sept 23/18 "CJ"

As a contribution toward Reconciliation, Indigenous Minister Carolyn Bennett announced the Manitoba Metis Federation will receive **$154 million** from the Federal government. This funding will go to a group working toward "Self-Government". Negotiations started in 2016 to resolve a land dispute originating in 1870 when Manitoba became a province. Negotiated at that time the government was to set aside a 5,565 sq. kilometres section land for 7,000 Metis children.

Oct 6/18 "CJ"

The Federal government will pay $25 to $50 thousand to each '60s Scoop survivor.

Oct 15/18 "Frontier Centre"

Indigenous Affairs is unlike most government departments in the way that most other departments provide services to all Canadians. Indigenous Affairs provides services to only one individual group of Canadians but has jurisdiction of over **90%** of Canada's landmass.

Oct 18/18 "Frontier Centre"

In the early 1970s the Federal government selected and funded 4 Aboriginal representative organizations (AROs) to exclusively represent Status Indians. Indian Affairs would control programs and funding. Voices of people most directly affected by the relationship with Indigenous rights, recognition and implementation will not be heard.

Oct 27/18 "CJ"
Senator Murray Sinclair stated that Manitoba has 10,300 youth in the child welfare system, with 90% being Indigenous. Although some have flourished, the majority have failed due to being cut off from family traditions.

Nov 4/18 "Frontier Centre"
The Truth and Reconciliation report called for an increase in child welfare funding, establish National standards for child welfare agencies, keep indigenous children in culturally relevant homes and narrow the gap between indigenous and non-Indigenous children in the welfare system. The TRC report pretends to treat Indigenous people as being responsible thus putting all blame on historical events. Manitoba Indigenous people represent 10% of the population, yet 90% of the 11,000 children in care are Indigenous. The main reason being the drinking and drug lifestyles the parents. In 1967 a "Caldwell" report examined 8 rural and one urban Residential Schools in Saskatchewan, 80% of the enrolment was from Indian Agents removing children due to their parent's lifestyle for safety. Both the Federal government and Native activists have provided Indigenous people with excuses for their irresponsible behaviour, those being Residential schools, Colonialism and racism. Staggering amounts of money have been spent on Indigenous child welfare only to have it get worse, yet the TRC report calls for more money.

Nov 14/18 "CJ"
Newly formed Lubicon Cree First Nation in Little

Buffalo Alberta was created after being missed in in the Treaty 8 negotiations in the 1800s. The band has been fighting for a land claim since 1930. The band will receive 246 sq. kilometres of land and **$113 million** in federal and provincial funding.

Nov 14/18 "Crown Indigenous Relations and Northern Affairs Canada"
Carolyn Bennett announced that CIDC will launch a new "Implementation of Indigenous Rights Framework" (fully consistent with the United Nations declaration of the rights of indigenous people). The total workforce for CIRNAC 2018-19 is 3,108 full time people with a total budget of **$3.086 billion.**

Broken down
- Internal Services (management oversight, communication service human resources, financial management, information management, materials and requisitions): 1,231 full time people with a budget of $206,.679 million
- Rights and Self Determination: 1,021 full time people with a budget of $2.233 billion.
- Community and Regional Development: 856 full-time people with a budget of $646,678 million. Budgeted for amounts not allocated to specific core responsibilities (slush fund) for year 2016-17 was $6.4 million, for 2017-18 was $3.95 million, for 2018-19 and 2019-20 sums not available.

Commitments from the CIDC are:
- Starting in 2018-09 Ottawa will fund Indigenous participation and Treaty negotiations with non-repayable contributions as well as $51.4 million

over 2 years for participating in the "Recognition of Rights and Self Determination"

- Ottawa will fund $74.9 million over 5 years in support of a "Permanent Bilateral Mechanism" with Indigenous people (this will address the unique needs and priorities of each community).
- Ottawa plans to fully implement all 94 recommendations of the "Truth and Reconciliation Commission."
- Ottawa plans to pass discriminatory provisions under the Indian Act and will reinstate the rights removed from men, women and children (women stand to gain the most).
- Support stakeholders such as the Indigenous Tourism Association of Canada, Council for Aboriginal Businesses, Native Women's Association of Canada, Indigenous Works and continue to support large scale commercial and industrial projects through the "First Nations Commercial and Industrial Act"
- CIDC will fund development and modernization of Regulations for oil and gas on Reserve lands
- Invest $27.6 million to support climate change adaption (identify risk assessments, plan and implement measures, and flood plain mapping)
- Work with and support "Nutrition North Canada Indigenous Working Group"
- Support the "Northern Contaminants Program" (contaminants in northern country food)
- Invest 7.7 million annually to 60 communities to develop land use plans by 2021
- Fund $187.5 million toward "Active Management High Priority Contaminant Sites" plus an additional $50 million to clean up 35% of

contaminated sites posing an immediate health risk on Reserve lands.
- Fund $97 million for solid waste disposal sites.
- Target $112 million to set aside Procurement contracts for Indigenous businesses

Indigenous Services Canada (ISC)

The total workforce for ISC 2018-19 is 3,747 full time employees with an operating budget (prior to government funding and transfers) of **$9.420 billion.**

Broken down
- Internal Services: 695 full time people with a budget of $64.987 billion. For First Nation and Inuit Health 1,985 full time people with a budget of $3.092 billion.
- Well Being of Individuals and Families: 496 full time people with a budget of $3.343 billion.
- Community and Regional Development: 611 full time people with a budget of $1.825 billion.

Both CIRNAC and ISC advertise as being committed to become the employers of choice for Indigenous people

Nov 24/18 "Frontier Centre"

The Missing and Murdered Indigenous Women inquiry has asked for an additional **$50 million** over and above the **$54 million** already spent, as well as extended time. The Government has granted a 6 month extension. What is hoped to be achieved considering previous inquiries have already taken place? Recommendations from the previous inquiries toward police practices have already been adopted such as

(Cultural sensitivity training). The Manitoba Justice Enquiry and the Royal Commission on Aboriginal Peoples in 1996 stated that poor, addicted women on the margin of society fell into the category preyed upon by killers. Also stated was that Indigenous women were more likely to be beaten and murdered by their partners than non-Indigenous women. The overwhelming number of perpetrators are Indigenous men. After spending $ millions will the MMIW inquiry choose to blame, police, government, colonialism. These will have the root cause rather than put blame on dysfunctional families, communities where young girls are first victimized when children by family members and then later assaulted by abusive male partners, thus giving abusive men an excuse to continue abusing.

Dec 6/18 "CJ"

A **$600 million** Training School class action lawsuit has been given court approval to proceed. This will take in 13 facilities and be on behalf of living survivors as of Dec 8/15 and resided at any one of the training schools between Jan 1953 and April 1984. These training/reform schools were for boys and girls convicted of petty offences. The suit claims the schools were cesspools of sexual, physical and physiological abuse perpetuated by unsupervised and unqualified staff.

Dec 10/18 "CJ"

A coalition of First Nations want to move away from projects that are proposed and imposed on Indigenous people. Funded by the Federal and the BC, provincial government Indigenous businesses will move past impact agreements to initiative an ownership. The first project is to jumpstart the $300 million Kenny Dam water Release Project.

Dec 18/18 "CJ"
    Justin Trudeau publicly stated that he wants his relationship with Indigenous people to be his "Legacy"

Dec 21/18 "CJ"
    Metis and Non Status Indians launch a class action lawsuit after Carolyn Bennet stated after the original '60s Scoop payout that more work has to be done with the Metis and Non Status people. Bennet said they should not be made to wait any longer or suffer through more court battles.

Jan 9/19 "Frontier Centre"
    What had previously been the Indigenous Affairs Department and is now the Indigenous Services and Crown Indigenous Relations shows as having a **$10 billion** budget but neglects to have to show any transparency. Much money is buried in other departments therefore could actually be as much as **$20 billion**.

Jan 11/19 "CJ"
    Families of deceased Residential School survivors are suing the Federal government on grounds that the Chief Adjudicator had no right to impose a "signature rule" Some survivors were uncompensated due to passing away prior to signing an application.

Jan 18/19 "CJ"
    The United Nations Human Rights Committee ruled that gender rights persist in the Indian Act. The

Act violates 270,000 women and their decadents due to flaws. They ruled that women who lost their rights when marrying white men should have them reinstated.

Jan 18/19 "Frontier Centre"

Justice Patricia Hennessy stated the crown had failed to appropriately increase the **$4** annuity to every man woman and child. The 1850 "Robinson Huron Treaty" signed by 21 First Nations effected 30,000 Ojibway people. Today 3/4's of Canada's 750,000 its Nation people are eligible for that annuity. The Indian Act in 1876 froze the annuity payments at $4 to $5. In 2002 a creation of the Treaty Annuity Working Group took place (the Social Planning Council of Winnipeg). This group was determined that a modernized annuity would address chronic issues of poverty. The Prime Minister and Cabinet can increase annuities. In the 1840s Robinson Treaties were negotiated to ensure the future wellbeing, hunting, fishing and trapping on ceded lands.

Jan 19/19 "CJ"

The Thunder Bay Lakehead University will receive **$144,601** toward funding studies that promise to have a profound impact on relationship between Indigenous and Non Indigenous peoples.

Mar 1/19 "CJ"

The Liberal government is tabling Bill C-92 to give First Nations control over their child welfare system. Indigenous people hope to have this passed prior to the next Federal election. The Indigenous Chiefs want guarantees to have funding in place for things like parental programs, rehabilitative family services, substance abuse and warnings about fetal alcohol syndrome.

"Canadian Museum of Human Rights" Funded by the Federal, Manitoba Provincial governments and private sector donors, the cost of the Canadian Museum of Human Rights building in Winnipeg Man. was $351 million. Admission is $21 for ages 18 to 64, $17 for students and seniors and a complimentary no charge admission to Indigenous people with identification.

Mar 6/19 "CJ"
Justin Trudeau apologized on behalf of Canada for the mistreatment during the 1940 and late 1960 "Tuberculosis Crisis" A data base is to be set up for 9,000 files coproduce in-depth records of people transferred southern Canada during that time. The main objectives to allow for people to locate gravesites of relatives.

Mar 13/19 "CJ"
After stating "Canada is committed to righting historical wrongs", Carolyn Bennet announced settlement of a lawsuit for Indian day school survivors' suit originally filed 2009. Each former student will receive **$10,000.** Students who were the victims of physical or sexual abuse will receive **$50,000** to **$200,000.** Indian day schools began in the 1920s an estimated **200,000** attended. The class action suit will involve 120,000 to 140,000 people. School policies wouldn't allow children to speak their language and were forced to abandon their culture. Harm continued to be passed on through generations. This settlement will hopefully be a start to successful healing.

Mar 20/19 "CJ"

The liberal government in its pre-election budget has committed: **$1.2 billion** over 3 years. to enhance social services for Indigenous families and children. **$4.4 billion** over 5 years. to narrow the socio-economic gap between Indigenous and non Indigenous people. **$1.2 billion** over 3 years. to develop a long term approach for services for First Nation children. **$126.5 million** in 2020-21 to establish a National Council on Reconciliation to preserve the history between Canada and First Nation communities. **$337.7** million over 5 years. to create a commissioner for, and revitalize Indigenous languages.

Mar 25/19 "CBC News Calgary"

Bill Morneau, Canada's Finance Minister confirmed the Federal government is consulting with Indigenous groups about participation with the proposed Trans Mountain Pipeline. Discussions are also taking place as to possible equity and revenue sharing arrangements. Equity participation is considered as being an economic advantage to Indigenous groups on the project. A timeline to start will not be addressed until Stage 3 of consultations are completed.

Mar 27/19 "CJ"

Bill C76 passed 2nd reading. if passed this would commit the government to formerly adopt the United nations declaration on the rights Indigenous People.

Mar 27/19 "CJ"

Confederation College officially opened a smudging room inside the building. This is for use by elders and students for ceremonial purposes. An exhaust fan has been installed to remove the smoke after a ceremony and help to minimize/contain smoke that may defuse to adjacent areas. A smudge is the burning of sweet grass, sage, cedar and tobacco (referred to as medicine).

Mar 28/19 "CJ"

The town of Richmond Hill, Ontario rejected a proposal put forth by councillor David West to acknowledge the proceedings are taking place on lands held by Canada's Indigenous people. The deputy mayor stated that they were heading toward a course of political correctness that would be difficult to rein in, and that too much emphasis was being placed on one demographic. The motion was replaced with a proposal that all town employees be provided with education and training the history of Aboriginal people.

April 3/19 "CJ"

NDP health critic Don Davies requested that the RCMP investigate a coerced sterilization claim by dozens of indigenous women, saying they were pressured into sterilization. The Sask. Health Authority apologized in 2017 and an impending class action lawsuit followed. According to the RCMP after checking the National Data-base there were no filed reports on any related activities. Three Federal probes had previously been launched with similar results.

April 25/19 "CJ"

As an opportunity for Reconciliation due to climate change, the Tsilqhot"in First Nation has released a 1017 page review with 33 recommendations concerning British Columbia's firefighting practises. This will include infrastructure upgrades, sustained funding for firefighter training and a one stop reimbursement process for First Nations. Negotiations are underway for a request of **$211 million** over 5 years.

May 23/19 "CTV News"

Justin Trudeau officially exonerated Chief Poundmaker for a conviction of treason 134 years. ago. He stated the government acknowledges that Chief Poundmaker was a peacekeeper. In 1885, an expeditionary force attacked the tribe (for what they said was for looting), but were held back and forced to retreat. Poundmaker claimed they were gathering rations. Soon after he tried to negotiate a peace agreement but was arrested and sent to a Manitoba prison. He was released due to poor health and died 4 months later.

May 24/19 "CJ"

In pursuit of Reconciliation, Ottawa has committed **$100 million** toward a toxic clean-up of Nova Scotia's Boat Harbour effluent lagoons. Situated next to Pictou First Nation the Northern Pulp paper mill has operated since the late 1960s. This clean-up will help reconnect the Indigenous community with their traditional lands. The harbour had been used for recreation, food and harvesting ceremonial plants for medicine. This will end decades of trauma and start the healing process due to environmental damage. Nova Scotia had previously committed $100 million toward the clean-up and ordered the parent company "Paper Excellence" to stop effluent dumping by 2020.

Indigenous Infrastructure

Mar 23/17 "CJ"

Ottawa and Ontario will contribute **$1.6 billion** to connect 16 First Nation communities to the power grid. The "Watayninikaneyap Power Project" will be the largest First Nations–led and owned infrastructure project in Ontario.

April 23/17 "CJ"

Northern Heritage Fund Corp will invest **$2.2 million** to "Western James Bay Telecom Network" This is fibre optic installation to boost internet speeds in Fort Albany, Attawabistat and Kashechewan.

April 26/17 "CJ"

The Federal government has quietly promised Indigenous housing providers that live off-reserve a greater say in how money will be spread out. Ottawa has promised **$225 million** over 11 years.) this was forecasted in the 2018 budget. Over **50%** of Indigenous people live off reserves.

Nov 6/17 "CJ"

The Federal government is probing a "Social Finance Review." Ottawa is looking for a niche to unlock billions of dollars in private cash to help the homeless and boost incomes of Aboriginal people.

Dec 3/17 "CJ"

Two research reports costing **$245,000**

concluded that Indigenous people failed to file tax reports, due to them being difficult to understand (therefore missing out on low-income benefits).

Dec 17/17 "CJ"

Mattawa First Nations 9 member communities will receive **$240,000** in Federal funding toward a "Renewable Energy Readiness Assessment Project" expected to be complete by 2018. The most important aspect is to find a balance for the people between traditional activities and industrial development.

Feb 8/18 "Financial Post"

The newly formed National Energy Boards new review process must incorporate Indigenous knowledge and conflicts of interest into development of pipelines.

May 23/18 "CJ"

The Federal Government has set new employment quotas for federally-funded Infrastructure projects such as roads, bridges, water, and transit systems. Awarded businesses will be monitored and must employ Indigenous people, veterans and new immigrants.

June 17/18 "CJ"

Approximately **600** freezers/fridges are being replaced at a cost of **$1 million**. Little Grand Rapids and Pauingassi First Nation in Northern Manitoba were evacuated after a forest fire knocked out power. Food spoiled leaving the appliances unusable.

June 21/18 "CBC News"

The Metis Nation of Saskatchewan has signed a

historic agreement with the Federal government. "Metis Rights" will be implemented under the Canadian Constitution. This marks the beginning of negotiations to address issues such as rights to land and resources, education, self-government and preservation of culture.

July 3/18 "CJ"

Fort Severn and Peawanuk First Nation will receive **$6.2 Million** in Federal funding to upgrade transmission capacity. A new satellite system will be installed by "K-Net" a First Nations owned and operated internet provider.

July 18/18 "CJ" Grand Treaty 3

"Water Management Plan" will receive **$232,000** over 3 years. to combine Traditional Indigenous methods with "Western science" to monitor land and water over 28 communities.

July 28/18 "CJ"

First Nations Chiefs from Lake Nipigon Ontario are demanding more say in Lake Management, stating the government shouldn't be allowed to lower commercial fishing quotas while still allowing houseboat operations.

Aug 20/18 "CBC News"

The Federal government has announced a $1.9 million 20 unit building to be constructed in Halifax to support people with addictions and mental health issues. An additional **$150,000** will be provided to partner with the Mi'kmaq Native Friendship Centre in support of homeless people.

Sept 29/18 "CJ"

The Ochilchagwe Babigo inning Nation in Kenora Ontario will build a 5,000 sq. foot Economic Development Centre. This will house office space and an adult education and conference centre. The Federal government will fund **$1 million** on top of the previous **$500,000** commitment from the Kathleen Wynne government.

Oct 11/18 "CJ"

The Grassy Narrows Band opposes and will not allow timber harvesting on their 4,145 hectare Reserve. They state logging practices contribute to mercury contamination.

Nov 23/18 "CJ"

The Ontario Government will continue to fund the "Winter Roads Program with **$5.7 million.** This will supply 29 remote communities with 3,160 km of winter road access.

Nov 21/18 "National Post"

In 2017 the Federal government started an "Advisory Group" to develop a strategy for "social assistance" The fall economic statement announced **$755 million** over 10 years aimed at projects "not yet viable in the northern market" one possible program is to copy a program in Quebec which provides mortgage loans to residents of Indigenous communities. The ultimate goal would is to create a "Social Finance Market" that will not require ongoing Federal support.

Nov 23/18 "CJ"

Remote First Nations community airports will

require $ millions in funding for upgrades. Indigenous leaders say the lack of upgrades has caused needless deaths and suffering, spoiled food and medical supplies.

Dec 5/18 "CJ"

Environmental assessment is holding up the "Ring of Fire" mining development. Martin Falls First Nations band is leading a **$20 million** "Environmental Assessment" to determine the best route for the first 170 km of the "North South Route" over a 2-year period. The second phase will be for the next 150 km. Noront Resources, the company that is the key player in the development of the resource and has always favoured an East West road due to far fewer water crossings.

Dec 21/18 "CJ"

Pikangikum First Nation has become the first of 17 Reserves to be connected to Ontario's power grid.

Dec. 18/18 "Financial Post"

A Squamish First Nation community that rejected the Trans Mountain Pipeline has granted its approval of the Wood Fibre LNG pipeline. The community has a total membership of 4,000 people, 50% on-reserve and 50% off-reserve population. In return for its support the band will receive **$226 million** over the life span of the project along with a **$827 million** commitment to Aboriginal companies,

Dec 29/18 "CJ"

The Montreal Economic Institute presented a study "The First Entrepreneurs - Natural Resource Development of First Nations" This study stated that Indigenous oil sands workers earned an average of

$150,000 per year and the gas sector **$200.000** per year—in many cases tax free. The Canadian Association of petroleum producers published a report "Toward a Shared Future" stating over 6% of oil sands workers (11,900) are First Nations people. Indigenous governments received in the second half of 2017 **$55 million** in payments. In 2015-16 oil companies spent **$3.3 billion** in procurements from Indigenous owned companies.

Jan 2/19 "CJ"

Ottawa looks at the "Infrastructure Bank" to finance rural and remote broadband. To date the Federal government has pledged **$500 million** toward the broadband service. Ottawa created the Infrastructure Band in 2017 with 3 billion to help private companies invest in Canada.

Jan 17/18 "CJ"

The Bamlushawada Ltd. partnership with Nexbridge is waiting for approval for the installation of the East West tie line from Ontario's energy board. If approved the project will employ 600 construction workers, of which 250 will be First Nations people.

Jan 18/19 "CJ"

Wataynikaneyap Power, the Indigenous company connecting 1,800 km of transmission lines to 17 remote communities has now added additional communities to its joint venture. This brings it up to 24 Indigenous Community joint partners.

Jan 19/19 "CJ"

Cat Lake First Nation, a fly in Reserve of 500 has

declared a state of emergency due to mold, electrical problems and fire hazards. One complaint is the newer homes were built airtight with HVAC systems installed and the ban had no-one to maintain them, making the lifespan of a house less than 20 years. In Dec. 2018 a contractor was paid **$200,000** from the Federal Government to insect the 110 homes. Since 2016 Cat Lake received **$1 million** plus **$245,000** annually toward housing projects.

Jan 19/19 "CTV News"

Carolyn Bennet stated that in a "Manitoba Chiefs Report" addressed the fact that Indigenous people, businesses and governments contributed **$9.3 billion** into the economy in 2016

Feb 2/19 "CJ"

Work will be stepped up Cat Lake with the priority being to complete ongoing work on a nursing station and a 7 unit living complex.

Feb 20/19 "Net News Ledger"

The minister responsible for Families, Children and Social Development as well as Canada Mortgage and Housing Jean-Yves Duclos announced funding of a **$638 million** "Reaching Home Program" toward Indigenous housing. This is to address Indigenous homelessness in urban, rural and northern communities. Canada's National Housing Strategy/Community Housing Initiative" and the National co-investment fund will provide additional funding for Indigenous families currently living in community housing. The Federal government is working with Indigenous housing providers, organizations and other partners toward long term Indigenous housing no matter where they live.

Facts

The Reaching Home Program will receive **$413 million** over 9 years dedicated to Indigenous homelessness in urban centres. This is a 70% increase in funding.

This program will provide **$261 million** to maintain a community-based approach and address local priorities. It will provide **$152 million** toward priorities determined in collaboration with Indigenous partners over 3 years.

Canada's Housing Strategy will contribute **$225 million** dedicated to preserve and improve housing units for Indigenous families living in urban centres and cities across Canada. This program will provide Federal funding toward the Canada Community Housing Initiative which will support Indigenous households currently lining in community housing. It will provide **$25 million** for

• Indigenous housing providers through the National Housing Co-Investment Fund".

In the 2017/18 Federal budget **$600 million** over 10 years was allocated to support on-reserve housing as well as **$400 million** over 10 years. to support a "Metis Housing Strategy"

Feb 22/19 "CJ"

Cat Lake has signed an agreement with the Federal government for **$10.8 million.** This will be to supply 37 new portable housing units, as well as repairs and renovations to 21 existing homes. A temporary warehouse to store building materials will be constructed. Funding will be provided to train a housing manager. A follow-up agreement will take place concerning Elders, children and people with special needs.

Feb 27/19 "CJ"
     A two-day housing conference in Thunder Bay has brought in 300 people from Ontario, Manitoba, New Brunswick, Quebec, Nunavut and the NW Territories. First Nations "Housing Council and Technical Services Manager for the Independent First Nations Alliance" brought together First Nations house professionals, government and industry to meet and network housing initiatives. A presentation on chimney installation and maintenance was provided.

Feb 28/19 "CJ"
     Finances must be taught, Many Indigenous people after making their car payment have nothing left for a mortgage. Financial literacy is the key to home ownership. Bands should guarantee a mortgage. If you own your own home you will take care of it.

Feb 19/19 "CJ"
     Ashinawbe Business Professionals Association, will complement the Nishinawbe Aski Development Foundation which provides grants, loans, and support services to over 80 First Nations from Sudbury to Manitoba.

Mar 20/19 "CJ"
     The Liberals pre-election budget has committed **$4.5 billion** over 5 years to improve living conditions

for Indigenous people. This will provide Canada Mortgage Corp an additional **$100 million** to help organizations that provide so-called shared equity mortgages. Indigenous and non-Indigenous communities will take part in a **$2.2 billion** one time fund towards infrastructure projects. This fund is generated from the "gas tax"

Mar 27/19 "CJ"

Nishnawbe Aski Nation held a "NAN Environment Climate Change and Housing Symposium" with 100 participants over 2 days in Thunder Bay. Grand Chief Alvin Fiddler said housing has always been at the top of the list, referring to the Cat Lake mould crisis. In partnership with Ryerson University's "Together Design Lab" they will focus on housing design needs. Discussions were on seasonal change on winter road usability, waste management, health transformation and NAN homelessness.

April 1/19 "CJ"

A **$1.1 million** renovation to a 15-unit, Dryden Ontario apartment building has been completed. This will provide affordable housing for Indigenous Women and children.

April 6/19 "CJ"

The Federal government has pegged costs at $1.6 billion for Phase 2 of the Wataynikaneyap power project. Approved by the Ontario Energy Board this will connect 17 Remote NW Ontario Reserves with power as well as install a new power line to Pickle Lake. Work could start this summer with completion by 2023. Wataynikaneyap Power is majority owned by 22 First

Nations communities.

April 12/19 "CJ"

Indigenous Services Canada announced a **$36 million** "Innovation Program" for housing concepts that reflect Aboriginal culture, utilize traditional building techniques and emphasize energy efficiency. Up to 24 development concepts will receive **$6 million** with the remaining **$30 million** earmarked for the 15 concepts deemed worthy of being constructed.

April 23/19 "TB News-watch"

A proposed 58-bed complex in Thunder Bay will require a zoning bylaw amendment. Ontario Aboriginal Housing Services based out of Sault Ste. Marie originally proposed a 20 bed **$3.6 million** transitional home for Indigenous youth with programming services provided by the Thunder Bay Indigenous Friendship Centre. The new proposal calls for a 58 bed complex complete with a community centre, kitchen, dining room, offices, courtyard and smoking area. A 2018 survey showed that 2/3 of the 500 homeless people in Thunder Bay are Indigenous of whom 40% are under 34 years of age.

Indigenous Education and Employment Opportunities

May 7/17 "CJ"

An Indigenous Pipeline Course will be instructed by Ionotech Alberta. The course will support training in pipeline inspection techniques, pipeline operation and safety.

Oct 12/17 "CJ"

The Federal government is pondering options for the "Indigenous Job Strategy" **1.7 Million** people were registered in 2016 as being Aboriginal **(4.9%)** of Canada's population. It is estimated that in the next decade 400,000 people will be added to the present 900,000 Indigenous people of working age.

Nov. 7/17 "CJ"

Thunder Bay grade 7 and 8 students were given an insight on the Robertson Superior Treaty, by Indigenous Elders. They stated that the treaty (was a promise and an agreement)

Nov. 17/17 "CJ"

Ontario is to allow Indigenous post-secondary Institutions to independently grant diplomas.

Dec. 17/17 "CJ"

Bamkuwada, a corporation owned by 6 north shore First Nation communities, has a 30% stake in the construction of the East-West Transmission Line. The project is said to cost $777 million and the corporation hopes to receive the maintenance contract worth $500 million.

Supercom, a subsidiary of Bamkuwada has arranged with Confederation College to train 250 Indigenous people for construction and permanent jobs related to the transmission line.

Jan. 23/18 "CJ"

Jane Philpott stated **44%** of on-reserve Indigenous students of ages 18 to 24 completed high school compared to **88%** off-reserve. She also stated there are currently **140** federally funded education projects underway, benefitting 120 First Nation communities.

Aug. 8/18 "CJ"

"Camp Loon" a National Youth Program conducted by the Canadian Armed Forces teaches life skills to Indigenous boys and girls of ages 12 to 18. **Camp staff of 101 people** (Canadian Rangers, Canadian Armed Forces regular and reserve members). To date 1,000 Indigenous youth have been instructed. In 2018 they will host another **163 participants** from 21 remote First Nation communities.

July 25/18 "Nation Talk"

Patty Hardju announced a new job training program for **270** First Nations adult and youth to get into skilled trades. "Kenjgewin Teg Education Institute"

(Mshilgaade Miikan/ the path is clearing) The Union of Northern Ontario Indians and the Sault College joined in partnership and will receive **$2 billion** over 5 years and **$400 Million** per year ongoing to create a the new Indigenous Skills Training Program. This will also provide Indigenous people with "work placements and Canada summer jobs" Over the next 37 months KTEI will receive **$4.9 billion** in funding through the "Skills and Partnership Program" to enhance employability, labour market readiness for Indigenous youth. This will encompass skilled trades, hospitality, tourism, and teacher education. The "SPF fund" receives **$50 million** per year and to date has received **$250 million** (cash in kind) since inception. The Federal Government is presently working with Indigenous partners to co-develop and implement the new "Indigenous Skills and Employment training Program (ISET). Budgeted for 2018 is **$2 billion** over 5 years plus **$400 million** annually and will take a distinctions based approach to better meet the needs of First Nations, Metis, Inuit and "urban non-affiliated Indigenous people" Budget 2018 will also fund **$448.5 million** over 5 years to the "Indigenous Youth Employment Strategy". This is to support high quality (paid) work experience for young Indigenous students through the "Canada Summer Jobs Program"

Aug. 13/18 "CJ"

Approximately **335** Indigenous youth from the Sioux Lookout Region of NW Ontario will have job training over a 3 yr. period. A **$5.7 million** program funded by the Federal government will help students prepare for the workforce.

Aug 20/18 "CJ"

Wataynikaneyap Power, "the Indigenous consortium" is the contractor on the First Nations led project connecting power to 17 remote First Nation communities. The company has conducted an Indigenous "Line crew Ground Support Program" with 7 people graduating. One more course for 2018 and 2 courses in 2019 will take place.

Aug. 24/18 "CJ"

Members from 19 northern First Nations communities conducted a "Teach For Canada Program" this program is meant to recruit, train and support teaching positions in northern communities. 47 teachers took part in the 3 weeks of training in Thunder Bay. This program has a mandate to hire with-in the Sandy Lake First Nation.

Sept. 2/18 "CJ"

A "Natural Resources Youth Employment Program" saw **54 Indigenous youth** attend the 6-week course. They received education, training and shown work opportunities in the Natural Resources Management field. The "Partners of Youth Employment Program" hosted by Confederation College and Lakehead University w**ill see students obtain 2 high school credits as well as a pay cheque.**

Sept. 2/18 "CJ"

Residential Schools ran from 1960 to 1996. Government Records show that the majority of First Nations children were never enrolled in them. A 2012 report from the Edmonton Journal stated that out of Indigenous children aged 4 to 21,17,954 had completed a high school education on Reserves, 11,699 (**39%**) dropped out.

Aug. 23/18 "CJ"

An "Aboriginal Youth Leadership Program" will see 30 students aged 8 to 10 attend Mino Bimaadiziwin (leading a good life) course. The program focusses on life skills and leadership. This will take par at the Fort William Historical Park.

August 29/18 "CJ"

A "Call to Action" by the Truth and Reconciliation committee wants all colleges and universities to reduce barriers for Indigenous people. Libraries will ultimately rewrite all books that contain the word Indian and replace it with the word Indigenous.

Sept. 6/18 "CTV News"

A First Nations school celebrates a grand opening in Winnipeg. This will accommodate 156 students in grades 10 through 12. The school houses classrooms, a special needs resource room, a power mechanics classroom, a gym and student residences. The Federal government contributed $10 million toward construction and Indigenous Services Canada will contribute $5.6 million annually.

Oct 21/18 "CJ"

Federally funded "Anishenabek Employment training Services"(AETS) is to be replaced in 2019 with the "Indigenous Skills and Training Program" The program will have **600** points of service across Canada. This will provide Indigenous skills and training for youth, access to child care, programs for those with disabilities and programs for Urban Indigenous people. Another federally funded program will start in 2019. The "Dinoigehmin Aboriginal Youth Leadership Program" (AYLP) will teach participants culture, spiritual, mental, physical and wellbeing.

Oct. 10/27 "CJ"

Indigenous culture is being implemented in a "Land Based Learning Links Curriculum" held in Regina and Winnipeg. This will be a split course teaching subjects such as hunting, fishing, how rain soaks into the ground and how plants grow.

Dec 5/18 "CJ"

Thunder Bay public schools human rights advisor, Mihejabeen M. Abraham spoke to students about young people standing against gender violence. At the same workshop a presentation "Traditional Indigenous Culture" was presented by Marco Pasinelli. He stated that it was not in the Indigenous culture to be violent, differences were settled through talk. It was colonization that brought in the concept of women as property and subjects of men. Marco manages the "Kizhaay Anishinaabe Assault Intervention Program"

Dec 13/18 "CJ"

Mattawa Learning Centre opened its school in Thunder Bay, boasting that it is the first Indigenous tuition based non-government funded private school. Providing access to 200 students it has, classrooms, multipurpose rooms and an Elder resource area. The next phase will have living quarters, meals and 24 hr. supervision. the final phase will see a gymnasium.

Jan 19/19 "CJ"

Ottawa is planning a new approach in providing First Nations elementary and secondary school students with a more predictable stream of money. The parliamentary budget estimates that $336 to $665 million will be required to provide on-reserve youth a comparable education to off-reserve youth. Ottawa will fund **$1,500 per student annually towards language and cultural programs.** On reserve full day kindergarten will be provided to children of ages 4 and 5 Community education will now be within the jurisdiction of the Chief and Band Council. Ottawa will fund **$1.8 billion** in 2018-19 and up to **$2 billion** 2020-21.

Jan 19/19 "Wataypower News"

Wataynikaneyap Power owned by a 24 First Nations community partnership will install 1,800 km of transmission lines to Northern reserves. They along with Opiikapawiin Services Ltd. (infrastructure, health and safety association, Power-tel and OskiPimache-O-Win. The Wenjack Education Institute partnered with the Federal government's "Skills and Partnership Fund" is supporting a "line crew ground support training program" for Indigenous people.

Jan 26/19 "CJ"

Researchers from T. Bays Lakehead University will receive **$144,601** from the Federal government to study "profound impacts on relationships between Indigenous and Non Indigenous peoples"

Jan 26/19 "CJ"

The International Labourers Union will receive

more than **$181,000** toward a mobile classroom to reduce geographical barriers to Indigenous communities. They will conduct skilled trades training for construction craft worker and cement finisher.

Feb 19/19 "CJ"

At the UN "International Year for Indigenous Languages" Statistics Canada reported that only 263,840 people were able to speak an Indigenous language in 2016. MP's in Ottawa have agreed to have interpreters available in the House of Commons for 60 Indigenous languages.

Feb 19/19 "CJ"

Nishnawbe Aski Nation Chiefs held a special 2 day "Chiefs Assembly" to discuss the direction of Indigenous education. Grand Chief Alvin Fiddler stated "our kids shouldn't have to leave home to attend school" Indigenous schools should have a standard curriculum but also include language, culture, ceremony and traditional practices of hunting and fishing.

Mar 9/19 "CJ"

The Nokiiwin Tribal council will receive **$2.2 Million** from the Federal Government to implement Bill C-65. Funded though the Employment and Social Development, "Canada's Workplace Harassment and Violence Prevention Fund" This will provide funding for a 2 day workshop in Toronto to review new legislation to protect employees from harassment and violence in federally regulated workplaces.

April 1/19 "CJ"

Students at Thunder Bay's Bishop EQ Jennings

grade 7 and 8 class took part in a 4-week powwow dance fitness program. The Indigenous liaison stated that for the non-indigenous students it is a chance tolerant about powwows, Anishinaabe culture and history.

April 5/19 "CJ"
Students enrolled in the Native Child and Family Care program at Confederation College in Thunder Bay thanked people and businesses for their support toward the program.

April 6/19 "CJ"
Funding of **$93,500** from Indigenous Services Canada has been provided to the Northern Nishnawbe Education Council for the purchase of 5 Nissan passenger vans. These vans will be for the Pelican Falls High School in Sioux Lookout Ontario which provides living quarters and educates many students from Northern Reserves. These vans will be used to transport students to medical appointments, sporting events and field trips. The students will now be able to enjoy some of the cultural attractions others get to enjoy. Students took in a hockey game and went bowling in Dryden On.

April 18 and 22/19 "Northern Ontario Business News"
The newly established Anishinaabe Business professional Association will host its First three day matchmaking session in Thunder Bay June 10-12. The aim is to provide Indigenous entrepreneurs and non-Indigenous businesses to make roads into the supply chains for Northern Ontario and will "harness the power of Indigenous people in our region. Stating that "all projects are on our First Nations traditional lands" it

is time we tapped into these opportunities. The objective is to create opportunity for Indigenous businesses and communities in the mining, forestry, energy sectors and supply chains.

May 14/19 "CJ"

A Federally funded "Natural Resources Canada Program" has earmarked **$400,000** over 6 years toward training Indigenous youth considering a career in the clean energy sector.

Indigenous Heath

April 13/17 "CJ"
The Provincial and Federal governments will equally contribute **$5 million** toward establishing 19 new "Mental Wellness Teams" for First Nations.

May 27/17 "CJ"
Indigenous groups will share **$3.2 million** towards putting a stop to human trafficking.
- Fort Frances Tribal Area Health Services $291,392
- Ontario Native Women's Association of Thunder Bay $1.8 million
- Kenora Sexual Assault Centre $506,000
- Beendigen Inc. Women's Shelter of Thunder Bay $506,000
- Nishenawbi Aski Nation $170,000

May 24/17 "Toronto Star"
The Ontario and Federal Government has promised to transform health care for 48 First Nation communities by putting an end to a Colonial health system. The announcement follows the 4 youth suicides on the Pikangikum First Nation. Kathleen Wynne pledged **$1.6 million** for 20 full time medical health workers, with an aim to give Indigenous people more input into programs. In 2016 the federal government pledged **$69 million** over 3 years for "Mental Health

Emergency Programs" of which **$4.4 million** will fund a "Choose Life Initiative"

Nov 22/17 "CJ"

Nishnawbi Aski First Nation is attending a 3-day conference "Early Years Summit, Talks Healthy Children". This Summit is to address Equitable Services for First Nations children.

May 14/18 "CJ"

The Canadian Diabetes Association stated that 20% of on-reserve residents and 5% of off-reserve Indigenous people are affected with type 2 diabetes, compared to non-Indigenous people.

May 14/18 "CJ"

An Indigenous family has won a court case against the Federal government for **$110,000** over a **$6,000** set of dental braces that the government agency said they were not entitled to claim.

June 2/18 "CJ"

The "Beendigan Anishinaabe Women's Crisis Home and Family Healing Agency" opens its 4th location in Thunder Bay. This will be home to the "Healing Our Own" counselling unit. With the migration of Indigenous people to Thunder Bay there comes an increase in issues stemming from Colonization and Residential schools.

June 20/18 "CJ"

Approximately 1 out of 5 on-reserve families (many in poverty) are missing out of lucrative payouts from the increases in "Child Benefit Funding". This is mainly due to not filing tax returns.

Aug 7/18 "CJ"

Indigenous Services Minister Jane Philpott has committed **$68 million** over 3 years to Indigenous Saskatchewan, Manitoba and Ontario toward "Health Changes" aimed at giving First Nations more control of services closer to home. This will help in areas such as diabetes and infectious diseases.

Oct 11/18 "CJ"

The provincial "Talk Healing Line" originally set up for Northern Ontario Aboriginal women will now be expanded across the province. The 24-hour help line is to promote the health and well-being of Indigenous women. This will provide 129,000 women help in 14 languages. Records show 2,000 calls were received in 2017. "Beendigan the Indigenous provider receives **$500,000** annually and also receives additional funding to provide shelter to approximately 20,000 Indigenous Women and children experiencing violence.

Oct 11/18 "CJ"

An Indigenous teen who died in 2016, suffering from addictions did not receive proper help from social workers, school officials and others stated Daphne Penrose a Manitoba advocate for "Children Youth". Issuing a 104-page report stating the 17-year-old boy was let down. Also, in 2005 an Indigenous teenage girl was beaten to death by the mother and her boyfriend after repeatedly falling through the cracks of the Child Welfare system.

Nov 17/18 "CJ"

After an 11-day visit to Canada, United Nations Danius Puras stated that Canada's health system is commendable but still lacks in notion that health is a human right and that barriers still remain for Indigenous people, poor, undocumented migrants and vulnerable groups.

Nov 22/18 "CJ"

For a 3rd consecutive year, 21 First Nations youth will meet with Prime Minister Trudeau, members of the cabinet and senate to discuss the need for a federally funded "Northern Child Care Advocate, drinking water, education, mental health and food sovereignty. This same group will head to Australia to attend the 2nd National Aboriginal/ Torres Straight Islander "suicide prevention conference"

Jan 18/19 "CJ"

Esksoni First Nation, Nova Scotia's largest Mi'kmaq reserve is in a "mental health crisis. Multiple suicides, drug overdoses, and alcohol related deaths have taken place in the last 2 weeks. Poverty, trauma and addictions passed down from previous generations are a factor. On-reserve clinical support and counselling are required due to "racism and discrimination" existing if reserve members must travel to towns to access help.

Jan 19/19 "CJ"

Thunder Bay District Health Unit held a 3-day gathering to explore First Nation community food plans, diabetes and obesity (all of which are the impact of racism).

Jan 9/19 "CJ"

A three-day Nishnawbe summit "Building Upon Our Strengths" in Thunder Bay was to find best practices in the health field. This is the 2nd annual summit to inform people that they have to be responsible for their own health.

Mar 21/19 "CJ"

The Liberal government in its pre-election budget has committed; **$220 million** over 5 years. to Inuit children who face unique challenges to get health and social services due to remoteness.

April 20/19 "CJ"

A federally funded **$18 million** Health Centre on the Kitchenuhamaykoosib Inninuwug First Nation has officially had its grand opening. It will, unlike other centres, be equipped with a pharmacy. This will provide accessible, culturally appropriate heath services and mental health care for the approximately 1,000 Ojib-Cree living there. The Reserve is 400km NE of Sioux Lookout accessible by air or winter road.

Indigenous Justice

Mar 7/17 "CJ"

A one-day conference was held in Thunder Bay to develop a "First Nations Core System" based on their traditions. In attendance was Akwesasne Court, New Brunswick Healing and Wellness Court, First Nation Court of New Westminster, Tribal Court System USA and the Indigenous Peoples Court of Thunder Bay.

Mar 9/17 "CJ"

Justin Trudeau says more must be done to help Indigenous youth. This came with a meeting of Colton Bushiest family. Trudeau stated "we as Canadians must do more." This came after Gerald Stanley was acquitted in the shooting death of Colten Boushie.

Mar 10/17 "CJ"

The "Broad Based Safer Ontario Act" will fund the North American Police Service with **102 million** in 2017 plus an additional **$189 million** over 5 years.

Mar 18/17 "CJ"

Letter to the Editor: A letter was sent criticizing how Natives must start holding themselves accountable for their behaviour to each other if they expect white people to be accountable for racism. The author asked to have their name withheld due to personal safety or backlash.

April 19/19 "CJ"

Colten Boushie's family speaks at the United Nations "Permanent Forum on Indigenous Issues" in New York. The family spoke of Colten's death and the families experience with the police and courts.

April 29/17 "CJ"

Kenora, Toronto and London are to be home to "Bicultural Community Justice Centres" These Centres are to tackle the overrepresentation of Indigenous people in the Criminal Justice System. This is to create alternatives to incarceration, taking in factors such as homelessness, poverty, mental health and addictions, into consideration. These people face challenges resulting from Intergenerational trauma and colonialism. Healing should take place in a community setting but will still parallel the criminal justice system.

Dec 13/17 "Frontier Centre"

A 1996, 4,000-page report from the "Royal Commission of Aboriginal Peoples briefly describes violent death and cannibalism, occasional warfare among the Iroquois, the lethal conflicts of the Blackfoot and buries west coast pre-contact slavery. Similar activities are now viewed as crimes against humanity, ethnic cleansing or genocide. These events took place over things like possession of territory, elimination of military threats, slavery, forced labour, sexual exploitation, trade or status enhancement.

Dec 2/17 "CJ"

Harold Johnson, a Native Cree from Treaty 6 Territory in Saskatchewan published a book called Firewater. Johnson a graduated lawyer from Harvard and Crown Prosecutor wrote with the focus on how alcohol is killing his people. He states Manitoba presently has more Indigenous children in chid care than in the 60's. In his book he questions how can Manitoba stop Fetal Alcohol Syndrome when irresponsible parents won't stop drinking? He also questions why Indigenous leaders are so vocal on some issues but fail to address the real problem? If alcohol and Native are used the same sentence it is racist. Harold estimates that 50% of his people from Treaty 6 have die directly or indirectly from alcohol. In his research he found that 30% of Indigenous people don't drink. He stated that everything from the 60's scoop, child welfare, the racist justice system, overrepresentation in jails, missing and murdered women and communities with suicide epidemics should all be blamed on irresponsible parents drinking. In a final statement he said maybe Elders were right when the Treaty 6 negotiations took place an absolute ban on alcohol was to happen in their Territory. This was later struck down by the Supreme Court.

Dec 30/17 "CJ"

The Court ruled that an Indigenous American Hunter had the right to harvest an elk near Castlegar British Columbia on the pretence that he was exercising his constitutional rights for ceremonial purposes.

Feb 1/18 "Frontier Centre"

Canadians seem to be caught in a soft racism trap, with low expectations when it comes to Indigenous people. For some reason people are being convinced that Indigenous people should be treated differently than every-one else. Syrian refugees are given help on a temporary basis but expected to make it on their own. There are many special federal programs available only to Indigenous people, regardless of their income level. This is based on a subconscious belief that all Indigenous people need our help. You take away people's independence and pride, by putting them in a separate category and treat them like victims.

Feb 27/18 "Frontier Centre"

Statistic Canada says Indigenous women and girls are 3 times more likely to be at risk of violence than non-Indigenous females. Why is it that Chiefs, organization advocates and the media concentrate so heavily on the non-Indigenous perpetrator? A 2013 RCMP report stated that the majority of abused or murdered Indigenous women and girls took place where the abuser or killer was an Indigenous man that was also an acquaintance or family member. Chiefs and the media want people to believe racism is the main culprit, when it is actually Canada's dysfunctional Reserve system at fault. Mar 1/18 "Frontier Centre" Politically after Gerald Stanley was acquitted of Colin Bushie's death a review of jury selection was made Canada's Justice Minister Jody Wilson-Raybould and Justin Trudeau tried to impose a quota on the number of Indigenous jurors required if an Indigenous person is charged with a criminal offence. To alter the system due to race was rejected by the Supreme Court. One of the criteria to become a juror is having no criminal convictions. There is no proof that jurors of the same race are impartial. It is the right of the accused to be tried by a jury of his peers, not the right of social groups.

April 1/18 "CJ"

Nelson House First Nation mourns the death of 3 boys ages 11 to 13. The youth were walking and riding bikes when struck by an Indigenous drunk driver on the Reserve.

May 11/18 "Frontier Centre"

The Justice Minister Jody Wilson-Raybould said that there aren't enough Indigenous people selected for Jury duty. After the acquittals in the murder trial of Colten Boushie. Many said that the outcome may have been different had there been Indigenous jurors? However Tina Fontain's murder trial did have Indigenous jurors and the outcome was an acquittal to charges.

May 24/18 "CJ"

Based on recommendations from the Truth and Reconciliation Committee, the Regulatory Body for Ontario's lawyers along with the Indigenous Bar Association has produced a 115-page guide to help legal professionals better understand legal rights, history and culture of Indigenous people. June 18/18 "Global News" The RCMP's "National Investigative Standards and Practices Unit" will receive **$9.6 million** over 5 years. to review police practices and policies regarding their relationship with Indigenous people.

June 1/18 "Washington Post"

The Chief Justice of Canada's Supreme Court stated the overrepresentation of Indigenous people behind bars is unacceptable. Indigenous people makeup 5% of Canada's population but represent 27% of the prison population. Indigenous youth represent 46% and Indigenous women represent 43% of people in jails according to 2016-17 Statistic Canada reports.

June 10/18 "CTV News"

The "Canadian Femicide Observatory for Justice and Accountability" established in 2017 is located at the University of Guelph's "Centre for the Study of Social and Legal Responses to Violence" This group stated that out of the 78 girls/women killed in Canada last year 12 were Indigenous.

June 11/18 "CJ"

The Justice System targets Indigenous people with impunity. 50% of all youth in jail are Indigenous. 98% of girls in Saskatchewan jails are Indigenous. 80% of girls and boys in Manitoba jails are Indigenous. 43% of women in jails are Indigenous. Indigenous people only represent 8% of Canada's population. Contributing factors are colonialism, cultural genocide, 60's scoop, inadequate housing, boil water advisories and decades of abuse from settler governments.

June 12/18 "Frontier Centre"

The Federal Government is set to have an expanded set of separate laws for Indigenous people for all times. The majority government has passed legislation that will as "Justin Trudeau" stated make it virtually impossible for future governments to change. This is to be a carry-over of the Indian Act which hampers Canada's economic progress and also adds to a cumbersome and expensive system. The changes will give Chief's more power and money to keep the Indian Act in place. Indigenous people will continue to be considered property belonging to the Tribe, rather than how all other Canadians are treated as individuals.

Pierre Trudeau tried to abolish the Indian Act and believed that all Canadians should have one set of laws regardless of ethnic origin and regardless how long their ancestors lived in the country. His plan was to abolish the Act and compensate people for lost rights. This was defeated by the Native Chiefs. Since then the failed Reserve system remains in place and Ottawa continues to write checks to the Chiefs with few questions asked. This system fails to solve the problems of chronic Indigenous poverty. Reconciliation means breaking down the barriers that divide people and not build new ones.

June 25/18 "CJ"

Statistics Canada showed that in 2016-17 46% of youth admitted to Correctional Devices were Aboriginal. Of Canada's youth population only 8% are Indigenous. This is systematic racism states one Manitoba activist. Punishment for offences should take into account poverty, unemployment, poor housing, addictions and mental illness.

June 28/18 "CJ"

Richard Wagner, Canada's Chief Justice, stated 25% of all people in jail 2015-16 are Indigenous. Canada's "Federal Prison Service" has failed to ensure physiological assessment tools were not fair to Indigenous people.

July 27/18 "Frontier Centre"

The "Right to Defend" shows the limited rights Canadians have. In the cases of Gerald Stanley and the Kil case (both men killed Indigenous intruders) were acquitted for defending their property. Since then the

RCMP has put property owners on notice, saying "If Invaded Return to Your House" under no circumstances are they to try to defend themselves or their possessions. If an invader dies, the property owner will be charged with murder if this advice is ignored.

Aug 11/18 "CJ"

A hearing is to take place as to whether a murder trial will proceed for Braydon Bushby in the Jan 2017 incident where a trailer hitch was thrown from a truck, striking and later killing a pregnant Indigenous woman.

Aug 28/18 "CJ"

Indigenous Minister Jane Philpott defended the transfer of a convicted murderer to a Healing Lodge. She stated that Healing Lodges are a way toward restorative justice for Indigenous people. The woman had been proven guilty in the murder of a 13-year-old girl by beating her to death with a hammer.

Sept 15/18 "CJ"

John Findlay a lawyer that oversaw the Caledonia class action lawsuit in 2011 is charged in a $1.5 million fraud case. Findlay was to oversee dispersal of funds in the Bands $20 million suit in the 2016 blockade of a residential developer on their traditional land.

Oct 11/18 "CJ"

Indigenous legal claims are impacting the federal finances. the "Contingent Liabilities Section" estimates that Ottawa will eventually have to pay out nearly **$20 billion** in land claims, 528 outstanding smaller claims, thousands of cases in litigation and Residential School claims. Lawyers for Indigenous people say it could reach

$80-$100 billion.

Nov 3/18 "CJ"

 Justin Trudeau apologized to the Tsilhoot Band for the hanging of 6 Chiefs over 150 years. ago. They were exonerated due to them acting as an Independent Nation when they attacked a road crew in their territory in1864.

Nov 5/18 "CJ"

 Ottawa will fund **$90 million** over 7 years to build and repair First Nations police stations. In the first 2 years. **$88.9 million** will be used to fund remote communities. This funding is on top of the previous **$291 million** over 5 years. toward improving salaries, hire additional police officers and equipment.

Nov 22/18 "CJ"

 Lakehead University's First Indigenous Dean of the LU Law School is suing the University for $2.6 million, alleging racial discrimination and constructive dismissal. The lawsuit states racism, micromanagement, opposition and hostility from some staff and students. The lawsuit is for loss of income, future income and benefits.

Dec 4/18 "CJ"

 Despite ongoing investments in the Indigenous Police Services, First Nations police spend most of their time going from crisis to crisis. Previously the federal Government committed **$291.2 million** over 5 years toward police services and programs, but no new money in the 2018 budget.

Dec 4/18 "CJ"

A Thunder Bay Police Officer has been taken off duty and being treated for exposure to bodily fluids. A 17-year-old, intoxicated Indigenous woman was videoed while being restrained on a stretcher by the officer and a paramedic. The video showed the officer striking the girl after being spat upon.

Dec 4/18 "CBC News"

Ottawa announces **$50 million** toward a gender violence program. Maryam Monsef stated 60 projects will receive as much a **$1 million** over 5 years. This is to support underserved groups (Indigenous women, LGBTQ2, Gender nonbinary, rural and remote areas). Paula Marshal director of Mi'kmaq Legal Support Network stated Indigenous women are 3 times more likely to experience violence.

Dec 5/18 "CJ"

Justin Trudeau publicly stated by recognizing the Indigenous rights that they have, it should prevent them from taking Canada to court.

Dec 7/18 "CJ"

The Thunder Bay Police Union state that Indigenous leaders were quick to show outrage when Chief Alvin Fiddler made the comment "there is no justifiable reason for violent and callous treatment for the police officer to striking an intoxicated Indigenous girl.

Dec 12/18 "Frontier Centre"

Healing Lodges conform to the philosophy that Indigenous offenders should be treated differently than others. The "Glade Case", a decision by the Supreme Court, declared that Courts must examine an Indigenous person's background differently than others (Gladue sentencing generally brings forth shorter jail terms). Healing Lodges began in the 1970s with the hope that using Indigenous culture with traditional healing practices in a welcoming atmosphere it will do a better job rather than incarceration. There is no evidence this works but why is it only available to Indigenous people if it does?

Dec 13/18 "CJ"

A 2 year-long review produced 206 pages and 44 recommendations toward the "systematic racism within the Thunder Bay police force." The Independent Review Director, Gerry McNeilly stated there is a "crisis of trust" between the police and Indigenous people. McNeilly also stated that "on many occasions there is far too much weight placed on the deceased people's level of intoxication"

Dec 20/18 "CJ"

A lawyer representing an Indigenous hockey team stated that "white teams got together in Manitoba and created a Junior B league which excluded First Nation's teams. - Dec 24/18 "CJ" MPP Patty Hajdu stated she would work with the Thunder Bay Police chief to implement 90 recommendations by Senator Murray Sinclair and the Truth and Reconciliation Commission. Hajdu stated "the safety security and well-being of Indigenous people is a priority of the Federal government.

Dec. 26/18 "CJ"

Judge Patricia Hennessy wrote that it is the Crowns duty to fulfill a treaty promise to increase monetary payments over time. This came after a delegation of 21 First Nations people filed a lawsuit over the $4 per member annual payment. There has been no increase in the annual payment since 1875. Anishinaabe people agreed to share their land in exchange for increased annuity if the lands generated money.

Jan 2/19 "CJ"

Thunder Bay is once again the murder capital of Canada with 7 homicides in 2017 and 8 in 2018. Charged with first-degree murder was Christopher Achneepineskum and accessory to murder Rachel Mary Moonias in the death of William Baxter. Charged with second degree murder was Charles Noman Carney in the death of a 65-year-old man. Amielia Corrie Sainnewap killed but no charges laid. David Hugh Sweeney killed no charges laid. Charged in the death of Ashley Chantel McKay were Marlene Lou Kwanddiaews, Terryl Nichol Irene Michou and Darren Steven Oombash. Charged with 2nd degree murder in the assault death of a woman was Peter Keeash. Geoffrey Corbell was killed in a suspected drug deal. Charged with 2nd degree murder was Johnathan Yellowhead in the death of Braiden Jacob (an Indigenous boy taking trauma counselling).

Jan 16/19 "CJ"

Thunder Bay City Council is studying a request from the Police Services for an additional $1 million on top of the $41.8 million allotted

Jan. 24/19 "CJ"

The "Level Indigenous Youth Outreach Program" introduced at the Kingsway Park school in Thunder Bay suggested that the justice system was unfair to Indigenous communities. Indigenous youth make up 8% of Canada's population yet represent 46% of prison incarceration. Jan 28/19 "CJ" Patty Hajdu stated in her monthly anti-racism column that Indigenous people represent 4.9% of the population yet represent 23.1% of the 2016-17 Federal Offender population.

Feb 19/19 "CJ"

Braydon Bushby will face a murder trail on Jan 21/19

April 23/19 "CJ"

The Federal government's "Colonial Model of Policing" which has received on average of **$160 million** per yr. under the Liberal government is failing according to First Nations. This program was set up for communities to administer their own policing or maintain discussions with the Mounties and/or RCMP.

Indigenous Climate Change

Dec. 18/18 "CJ"

Sara Cockerton, manager of Environmental Programs for Mattawa First Nations conducted a 3-day conference in Thunder Bay. The 60 members from 9 communities reviewed how they can adapt to climate change. Mattawa First Nation will oversee "Four Rivers Environmental Services" as they conduct studies on environmental challenges, watershed management, and climate change.

Feb. 19/19 "CJ"

The Federal government announced **$20 million** in funding aimed at reducing reliance on diesel. An all Indigenous panel will choose 15 communities to receive support in developing their own energy plans over the next 3 years. Nicholas Mercer an "off-grid specialist" says diesel generation costs approx. $1,500 per kilowatt hour versus solar and wind power that costs $7 to $8 thousand per kilowatt hour.

March 19/19 "CJ"

Seven Generations represented by 200 Indigenous youth held a "Transition in Energy Gathering" for 4 days in Calgary. Reviewed topics were alternative energy along with closely entwined energy subjects such as language, food self sufficiency, health, well being and housing. The group also requested that the federal government appoint an Indigenous Youth Representative.

March 19/19 "CJ"

Katherine McKenna, minister of environment kicked off a month long "Carbon Price Tour." She stated the government wants a program that isn't highly bureaucratic. Stating 90% of all money collected would be returned to people through income tax returns. 10% will go to small business, municipalities, hospitals, universities and Indigenous peoples.

April 18/19 "CJ"

Fourteen intervenors are in the top Canadian Appeals Court proceeding over the governments carbon pricing law. Amir Attaran a lawyer representing Northern Athebaska Chipewyan First Nations told the court that this law helps protect their Constitutional rights for hunting and fishing to which their very survival depends. First Nations agreed that a national response is critical, given the vulnerability of their people.

Author's closing remarks

What Canada needs is "true equality" for citizens. The present Government has enforced and is continuing to enforce hiring practices on government and private sector employers. By supposedly rectifying the issues we are often bypassing the best people qualified for the job. The only possible solution in this gender and race discriminated environment of today is to change human resources practices. A job application should not require your name, race or gender to be shown. Applicants should be short listed and hired due to qualifications.

By compensating historical pasts we are crippling the future of the country. Gender discrimination on the pay scale is relevant. An example is that women executives earn less than the males. We complain about what CEOs make in comparison to the average worker but is it better to raise the females pay or lower the males pay to what the average Canadian would consider reasonable income?

Secondary education presently is only provided free to certain groups. This benefit should be available to every student at no upfront cost. Progress of the students should be monitored to maintain ongoing eligibility in the system. All students after graduating or dropping out should have a percentage of their income be garnisheed to reimburse tuition costs, (whether the income is a welfare cheque, guaranteed income or a paycheque). A 12-month delay of payment could be offered for students to find work etc. This program would be self-sufficient in a matter of years and provide all people the same opportunity to excel in life. Certain groups are provided free living expenses and accommodation as well, this should be available to everyone or no one.

Non-partisan judges and Senators should be democratically elected. This would hinder the appointment of people to gain political dominance in Canada. The party in power should not have dominant control of the House Justice Committee or the Senate.

In order to make all Canadians equal, everyone's entitlements, and benefits should be based according to income. Approximately 95% of Canada's population either contributes or receives funding from the present tax system.

Accountability should be a requirement for all communities no matter what race, to obtain any type of government funding. An example being that a town or city must show open books and match government funding in some way to receive grants toward infrastructure projects. A large percentage of government income comes from the taxpayers (who deserve the right to know).

A government watchdog should be appointed to monitor attendance of Government officials trying to use public events for political gain. Justin Trudeau attended the service for the 7 immigrated children killed in a New Brunswick house fire. This was an unbearable family tragedy yet there was no attendance for the 13 hockey players killed in the Humboldt bus crash. If Government officials believe in attending parades or marches, costs should be born by them not the taxpayer. Another example of this is the recent attendance by Justin Trudeau in both the Vancouver Pride and Sikh parades he recently attended.

Canada spends billions on foreign aid to developing countries to promote democracy yet in our own country promotes a 2 tier Indigenous system. Status Indians, Inuit and Metis benefit from entitlements no matter what they have as income or where they reside. Not all Indigenous people attended Residential or Day schools yet every Indigenous person today is benefitting from Colonialism of the past. The educated and financially well off people will continue to benefit while the poor will continue to stay poor. These are the same people that publicize, and need poverty inflicted reserves to continue capitalizing on Federal funding. A 2016 Canadian census reported that there were 1,673,780 Indigenous people in Canada represented under the Indian Act, these people represent only 4.9% of Canada's population. Less than 40% of Status Indigenous people live on Reserves yet maintain many of the same tax advantages as those that do. Bands that are wealthy from "resource royalty" payments do not share their prosperity with poverty stricken remote reserves as other Canadians do via Federal regulated Provincial transfer payments. The First Nations Financial Transparency Act must be reinstated, or Chiefs and band councils will continue to have opportunity to filter money from the needy to benefit a select few.

Native language, culture, and tradition are becoming part of all Canadians education. Latin used to once be a dominant language in the world but it was eventually phased out of existence due to lack of use in the modern world.

Throughout my documents on Indigenous media coverage I've noticed constant numerical and percentage differences in coverage of similar articles.

With the millions of dollars spent on data collection from Statistics Canada and Indian Affairs how is it possible we don't have better recorded results?

Funding is being provided for duplicated programs with the same objectives that simply have a different sponsor name or business title. This is consistent in Indigenous education, social services, studies and employment programs. An example of this is the $20 million provided for 15 similar Indigenous communities to study alternate energy when one community could be the used, with the other communities learning and following from the research.

Why is a $2.2 billion one-time infrastructure fund from gas taxes being used for municipalities and Indigenous projects? when Status people are not required to pay gas taxes at reserve gas outlets?

All Status people should pay taxes the same as every other Canadian. If these people (through negotiated treaties) are not required to. This should be reimbursed with an income-tax refund at the end of the year. People shouldn't be allowed to take a photograph of an item being delivered to a reserve to capitalize on tax entitlements.

Justin Trudeau welcomed to Canada immigrants fleeing from persecution. Illegal immigration to which he reworded to irregular immigration has insulted all previous and hopeful immigrants that have and are abiding by the legal way to enter Canada. From day one all illegal boarder crossers should have been picked up and brought to a regular border crossing and processed appropriately. Any rejected immigrants should be deported in a timely manner. Why are new immigrants allowed to fast track their relatives through the immigration process? This allows over 50,000 immigrants per year to be fast tracked for a Canadian citizen sponsorship. The Liberals began this as a lottery system and then turned it into a first come, first-served program specifically for relatives.

Justin Trudeau, upon being elected, stopped Steven Harper's mandate to give the RCMP a timeframe to stipulate the difference between a hunting rifle and an assault rifle. He stating it required more time to be studied. After a 2 ½-year study where are we now with gun control?

Why are all Canadians tax dollars being used to provide rebates for electric cars when in many areas in Northern Canada it is an unavailable, uneconomical or inefficient use of transportation?

My views are not the same as everyone, but it is my hope only to make people think about how we are being taken advantage of. This governments wasteful spending of our tax dollars and lack of will to produce private sector jobs has set Canada backwards.

As shown through-out the chapters a majority of funding is spent on studies, committees and statistics, which have minimum value other than employing people.

Special thanks to Jeff Carlson for his help with editing and the designing of the book cover.

www.ingramcontent.com/pod-product-compliance
Lightning Source LLC
Chambersburg PA
CBHW020249290526
45784CB00003B/1173